Peter Walker

Minimalist Gardens

Essay and text by Leah Levy

Essay by Peter Walker

Graphic Design: Sarah Vance

S P A C E M A K E R   P R E S S

Washington, DC

Cambridge, MA

Laurie Fields

Front cover:
Plaza Tower and
Tower Center Park Fountain,
Costa Mesa, California
Photo: Pamela Palmer

Production Coordinator:
Susan McNally
Printer:
Palace Press/Hong Kong

Publisher: James G. Trulove
Spacemaker Press

ISBN 1-888931-01-9

Contents

Acknowledgments

I am indebted to a great number of people who have contributed both to the development of this book and to the lifetime of work and thought that is its subject.

First to my partners at Peter Walker William Johnson and Partners, Bill Johnson, Doug Findlay, Tony Sinkosky, Thomas Leader, David Walker, Jane Williamson, David Meyer, and Mia Lehrer; and to my immediate past partners Cathy Blake, Michael Brooks, and Martha Schwartz—without them neither the work nor the book would have been possible.

Also to the Peter Walker William Johnson and Partners staff since 1984:

Steven Abrahams, Wolfgang Aichele, Verda Alexandra, Duncan Alford, Tim Baird, Ka-t Bakhu, Arthur Bartenstein, Eva M. Bernhard, Claire Wrenn Bobrow, Charles Brandau, Dixi Carrillo, James Curtis, Andrew Day, Albert DeSilver, Kathryn Drinkhouse, Sara Fairchild, Andreas Flache, Joanna Fong, Philip Frankl, Marta Fry, Charles Gamez, Lisa Ganucheau, Alke Gerdes, Liette Gilbert, Marshall Gold, Elizabeth Gourley, E. Leesa Hager, Jane Hansen, Sandra Franzoia Harris, Tim Harvey, Chester Hill, Roxanne Holt, Kakiko Ide, Christine Jepson, Bruce Jett, Dirk Johnson, Mark Johnson, Kimberlee Jong, David Jung, Martin Kamph, Akshay Kaul, Ken Kawai, Esther Kerkmann, Rhonda Killian, Kazunari Kobayashi, Sonja Kurhanewicz, Grace Kwak, Shelby LaMotte, Patrick Lando, Randy Lein, Jaruvan Li, Quindong Liang, Lynda Lim, Henry Lu, David Madison, Esther Margulies, Anuradha Mathur, Alex Mena, Toru Mitani, Yasuhiko Mitani, Duane Moore, Susan Nettlebeck, Diane Nickelsberg, Makoto Noborisaka, Joseph Nootbaar, Sally Pagliai, Pamela Palmer, Lawrence Reed, Sandra Reed, Martin Rein-Cano, Kerry Ricketts, Dee Rizor, Robert Rombold, Lisa Roth, Gabriel Rustini, Mathew Safly, Yoji Sasaki, Doris Schenk, Kimberli Schumacher, Heidi Siegmund, Paul Sieron, Kenneth Smith, Carol Souza, Kimberlee Stryker, Margaret Stueve, Jane Tesner, Gina Thornton, John Threadgill, Randy Thueme, John Tornes, Nicholas Wessel, Stella Wirk, Christopher Yates, and Anna Ybarra. I deeply appreciate their efforts and their many contributions.

I am indebted to my mentors and teachers, Stanley White, Hideo Sasaki, Lawrence Halprin, and my longtime friend and role model Dan Kiley; and to the students at the Harvard Graduate School of Design and the SWA and PWWJ intern programs, who have greatly influenced my thought.

Over many years of practice, a group of clients, planners, and architects have become variously mentors, colleagues, and friends. They have encouraged, educated, and guided my work. I am indebted to Jerry McCue, Herman Ruth, Pietro Belluschi, Don Knorr, Ernest Kump, Chuck Harris, Art Sweetzer, Don Olsen, Chuck Bassett, Frank Gehry, Bruce Graham, Ray Watson, Art Hedge, Ed Killingsworth, Paul Kennon, Bob Frasca, Jim Freed, Arata Isozaki, Helmut Jahn, Yoshio Taniguchi, Paul Krueger, Kunihide Oshinomi, Ricardo Legorreta, Gen Kato, and Don Hisaka. I deeply appreciate their friendship, their inspiration, and their guidance.

Membership in two previous firms has been important to my development, and I would like to formally thank the then partners of Sasaki Walker and Associates: Hideo Sasaki, Richard Dober, Stuart Dawson, Ken DeMay, Mas Kinoshita, Kalvin Platt, Ed Kagi, Dick Law, Gary Karner, Gene Rosenburg, and George Omi; and The SWA Group: Kalvin Platt, Peter Bonet, Michael Gilbert, Ed Kagi, Gary Karner, Dick Law, George Omi, Peter Schneider, Ray Beknap, James Reeves, Tom Adams, Gerry Campbell, Willie Lang, Gene Sage, Terry Savage, Bill Callaway, Danny Powell, Wendy Simon, Loreen Hjort, Kevin Shanley, Mike Sardina, George Kurilko, Roy Imamura, Dirk Myers, John Wong, Ed Morgan, Don Thompkins, Eduardo Santaella, Jim Lee, Duane Neiderman, Susan Whitin, George Hargreaves, Rob Elliott, Dick Thomas, Doug Way, Fred Furuichi, Steve Calhoun, John Exley, Jim Roberts, Jim Culver, Ken Beesmer, Bill Miller, Walt Bemis, and Owen Peck. These firms provided the opportunity and the experience to participate in the great wave of post–World War II environmental expansion.

I would like to express special thanks to my remarkable publisher Jim Trulove for his continued enthusiasm for this project; to my patient and dedicated editor and friend Leah Levy, for her support and wisdom; to the multitalented and resourceful Sarah Vance for her insightful design of the book; and to the many inspired landscape photographers who have documented our work over the last forty years, especially Gerry Campbell, Allen Ward, David Walker, Pamela Palmer, Dixi Carrillo, and Tim Harvey. Jane Williamson, Sandy Harris, and Dirk Johnson provided invaluable and untiring assistance.

Finally, I want to thank my ever supportive and indulgent family: my wife, Martha, and my sons, Chris, Peter (JR), David, Jake, and Josie.

P. W.

In memory of Kate Walker

IBM Solana, Westlake and Southlake, Texas

Dialogue with the Land:

The Art of Peter Walker

by Leah Levy

Our contemporary categorization of the created landscape is consistently and specifically associated most directly with architecture. In that context, the landscape "architect" has been typically relegated to planner of the spaces around and between the architect's structures, which are the most discernibly visible monuments in the landscape. In contemporary universities, the disciplines of architecture and landscape architecture share the same departments, landscape having been shifted from an earlier association with agricultural and horticultural schools. Critically, the traditional vocabularies for discourse on the designed landscape and gardens are those that are meant for architecture or agriculture.

In considering the work of the landscape architect Peter Walker, conventional standards of evaluation of landscape architecture and gardens are limiting. Although Walker's mature work has focused on the "visibility" of the landscape through design, engendering his claim for the field as an independent entity with a place and status appropriate to the visual arts, performing arts, and architecture, the actual existing critical literature of the created landscape in comparison to that of the other arts is remarkably meager.

Indicators of Walker's style can be traced to disparate and yet logically connected sources. Archetypical and primitive vestiges on the land such as the Nazca Lines in Peru and Stonehenge in England demonstrate a basic and communal impulse to mark the land. An essential human urge to communicate with the greater environment, to signal an awareness of and quest for connection with earthly and celestial mysteries, and to allude to the power of the greater forces are evidenced in much of Walker's work. There are many instances when the work focuses on the enigmatic qualities of nature represented by the sound of water, the stasis and weight of stone, rustling changes by the wind, blocks and patterns of shifting color, shimmering and magical mists, and elusive light.

In a similar context, the classical order of seventeenth-century French gardens, especially those of Andre Le Nôtre, serves as strong precedent to individual elements of Walker's approach. His intuitive as well as intellectual affinity with patterns, rhythms, and order, and to a kind of Cartesian synthesis, is apparent throughout his work.

The influence of Zen gardens is also strongly apparent in Walker's work. An underlying philosophical distillation of the complex to achieve the simple is evidenced in both distinct components and the unifying wholeness of many of his gardens.

Walker's work is rooted as well in the progression of modern landscape history. As an individual he is consistently committed to illuminating and paying homage to the history of landscape design of his century.[1] The work of garden makers of the mid–twentieth century, especially Thomas Church and Isamu Noguchi, was particularly inspiring to Walker in his formative years. Nevertheless, to effectively reflect on the success and meaning of Walker's landscapes, their place in contemporary culture, and the persistent dialogue of his thinking and his work with art, an analysis of major artistic developments of the twentieth century is perhaps the most relevant and fruitful approach for the purposes of seeing this work in a current cultural context.

The early decades of the twentieth century were replete with innovations in art, science, and culture that were to dictate directions of investigation throughout the century. Central to a new perception was the pioneering of pure abstraction in the visual arts; that is, art that did not refer to or imitate any real or physical image, but, in its own independent and abstract form, served as the complete vehicle for expression and exploration. Underlying the geometric in much of this original work, especially that of the early Russian constructivists, was a striving to more directly access, reveal, and portray universal mysteries that humankind has always sought: ways to ponder and understand phenomena that one experiences but that cannot be explained with traditional depictions of reality.

Freed from the restraints of representation, two- and three-dimensional art could be approached as music is, for instance: without any intent to reproduce a specific, recognizable experience, and with a new freedom for the artist and observer to respond on a level beyond the conscious.

Another example of the inventive spirit of the early twentieth century is the work of the French artist Marcel Duchamp, who rejected the object (literal *or* abstract) for its beauty and meaning and extended the artist's realm into a nonretinal art of the mind. Duchamp claimed for the artist the right to designate what is to be considered art, broadening the arena for artistic examination. By blurring the edges of artistic categories and conferring the status of art on whatever non-art-like objects and ideas he chose, Duchamp created options for artists beyond the traditions of painting and sculpture that continue to be explored and to direct much artistic investigation today.

The breakthroughs of the abstractionists as well as the conceptual practices of Duchamp seemed to converge midcentury to form the historical roots, along with social, political, and cultural influences, of what came to be known as "minimal art." Since its most crucial years in the 1960s, minimalism, arguably the first truly American art, has become a loosely used catchall term absorbed into the culture to refer to styles that are nonfigurative, nonreferential, geometric, or merely of few and simple parts.

But the term *minimal art* was coined to refer to and identify a very specific point in time, approximately 1963–1968, and a small collection of individual artists working primarily in New York City, including Donald Judd, Dan Flavin, Sol LeWitt, Robert Morris, and Carl Andre. The artworks of these artists reflect a philosophical basis that eschews attempts at traditional categorization: the artists' major intent was to make objects that would occupy space and be perceived in physical proximity to the viewer's own body, also occupying space,[2] an "unreproducible communication."[3]

The materials as objects in space were the subject and content of minimal art and necessitated being perceived directly and experienced physically by the viewer. With a goal of arriving at the most direct way of making a primary object to effect a primary experience, the minimal artists sought a reductive method and result.

Because the "content" of the art *was* the relationship of the object and the environment to the viewer, these works were often considered penultimately "formalistic": they could be described well (size, shape, color) but could not be understood without the actual experience of walking around them, through them, next to them, and in them. Included in an open-ended array of formal traits of these works were the use of simple and geometric shapes, repetition and systematized placing of objects, modern materials and industrial fabrication, three dimensions (although meant to defy being perceived as sculptural), primary colors, and the placement of the structures directly on floors, leaning against walls, without pedestals or framing, and in immediate relationships to the space.

Another significant feature of the works of this minimal art period is the spaces in which they were placed and seen, whether in the "white cube" of the gallery or in the out-of-doors. Given that they were meant to point out the physical and phenomenological relationships between the objects, the human body, and the space in which they were placed, relative scale of all elements was often carefully considered and calculated.

While sharing the sensibility of the formalist aesthetic as exemplified by the work of the minimal artists, Peter Walker's work also seems to have equally powerful connections with other groups of artists of the twentieth century. These artists, whose work may have a look of systemic formalist abstraction that has been encompassed by the term *minimalism*, make artwork having quite a different philosophical premise. Including painters as well as object makers, such artists as Ad Reinhardt, Agnes Martin, Robert Ryman, Robert Mangold, Ellsworth Kelly, Porfirio DiDonna, Yves

Klein, Jasper Johns, and Robert Irwin aligned their abstractions with a more subliminal meaning. In some of these works, rhythms and repeated patterns refer more to the systems of organisms and the cadence of poetry (the repetitive nature of the tides, of the heartbeat, of ritualized motion) than to the mechanization of minimal art as a mode of indistinction and relational regularity.

Another realm of art that relates to contemporary art theory and practice is a broad-based body of diverse projects made out-of-doors by individuals often designated as land and earth artists. While these umbrella titles describe the work of artists using the out-of-doors as a large, unencumbered, noncommercial space without intending necessarily or specifically to make connections with "nature" (Robert Smithson's *Spiral Jetty*, the land manipulations of Walter de Maria, Michael Heizer's earth and rock works, and the works of Dennis Oppenheim and Robert Morris, for example), they also extend to artists who consciously make statements about the relationship of humankind to the environment and, sometimes, of nature to the poetic (Andy Goldsworthy's ice constructions and delicate twig webs, James Turrell's altered crater for celestial viewing, the light projecting and containing tunnels of Nancy Holt, Ian Hamilton Finley's classical garden markings, and the sculpted landscapes of Richard Fleischner).[4]

Artistic attention, by these artists and a diverse group of others, also focuses on works of a scale and an intent that address the public and urban landscape (Siah Armajani, Doug Hollis, Maya Lin, Richard Serra, Alice Aycock, Christo), and architecturally related design and installation (from Donald Judd's buildings, David Ireland's houses and walls, Gordon Matta-Clark's fragmenting of architecture elements to the furniture of Scott Burden). Some of this work exhibits commentary on "sophisticated" modern vision and intent; other work acknowledges its origins in a most primitive impetus to place rocks in a pile, pour water, and assert and probe the mysterious and inexplicable illuminations of nature.

Peter Walker's work is a hybrid of movements and styles, an investigation of the reservoir of essential qualities in the art of the century and his time that he plumbs for revelation. His affinities synthesize, in his unique vision and place, a body of work that doesn't "fit" into established categories or disciplines, and so we adopt the term he continues to use for himself: *landscape designer*. His work relates to the minimalists not because he can recreate or duplicate a crucial moment in the history of artistic thinking—have its look or make its objects—but because aspects of the visual and mental vocabularies of minimalism compare essentially with components of his own perspective.

Along with a strong commitment to the value of the abstract, the serial, and the geometric as means to accessing revelation in and through nature, Walker has also understood the potential of the characteristics of contemporary art movements to serve pragmatic and political purposes as a context for landscape design. Minimal art and earthwork applications of independent objecthood make the object/landscape visible, claim status and space, and extend the lexicon and sphere of elucidation for his working on the land. Always accepting beauty, Walker also embraces humor, commentary, subversion, pun, dialogue, collaboration and poetry. Underlying the nature of landscape design as Walker practices it is the possibility of eluding personal, professional, and artistic labels, and the goal of changing how we perceive and live in our world, and ultimately what we make of our planet.

Early Work: 1957–1977

Foothill College

Weyerhauser Headquarters

Concord Pavilion

IBM Santa Teresa

Sydney Walton Park

Foothill College, Los Altos Hills, California

Concord Pavilion, Concord, California, above

Weyerhauser Headquarters, Tacoma, Washington, left

Sydney Walton Park, San Francisco, California

Classicism, Modernism, and Minimalism in the Landscape

by Peter Walker

Classicism is defined by classicists as literally the study of classical Greece and its extension (revival), Rome. Each age of art historians, artists, and architects have redefined or further defined classicism to suit the purpose of their particular age. Various subcategories of classicism are labeled and judged by each age as good or bad (e.g., classic revival, neoclassic, etc.), and painting, sculpture, music, literature, and architecture have varying esoteric interpretations of the meanings of these distinctions.

However, there seems to be a general agreement that certain qualities are inherent in the classical ideal such as purity, clarity, expressions of humanity, origination from nature, and expressive derivation from craft or technique. By these broader definitions it is perhaps easier to see that a certain spiritual quality must be within a work or a period to qualify it as classical.

It is arguable whether modernism is, or was, a classical movement. Clearly, the early modernists thought so. In his 1923 *Vers une architecture*, Le Corbusier compares the great early works of engineering, the bridges and ocean liners, with Greek temples. It is hard for me not to see Mies van der Rohe in these same terms in spite of his romantic visual interests. And even his reductivist attitudes were not merely structural functionist inspirations. An ideal sense of beauty seems to always override the simply necessary. Even the modernist creed "less is more" can only be taken meaningfully in its ideal sense. Louis Kahn, too, in his quest for "what it wants to be" and in his passion for the movement of light seems classic, though the sense of weight in his work adds Romanesque overtones.

Classicism in modern landscape design is perhaps a less easily charted line. It might fairly be said that twentieth-century modernism itself has not yet been as fully realized in the design of gardens as that of buildings. However, I would argue that gardens became modern long before the architecture of the late nineteenth and twentieth centuries, for both in traditional Japanese gardens and in the formal gardens of the seventeenth-century French gardener Andre Le Nôtre, not only the true spirit of classicism but the beginnings of modernism seem apparent.

It is difficult to find examples of classical Greek or Roman gardens outside of written or drawn descriptions. There seem to be no formal or stylistic corollaries to the classical architectural orders. This is not to say that a generally agreed-upon vocabulary of gardens did not exist. The axes, allées, bosks, basins, canals, terraces, paths, parterres, meadows, and beds share with architectural elements most of the recurrent components of both classical and later gardens.

It is also clear that the garden was seen objectively as an element, though almost always as a part of architecture, defined by a building, a colonnade, or a wall. What is less clear is the way in which the general landscape was seen in classical time as separate from the created garden or from the farm or agricultural plot, which was often of necessity tended more carefully than are gardens today.

I have learned most of what I know about gardens through intuitive investigation because, unlike scholarship, practice and teaching are basically nonlinear enterprises. As a late second-generation modernist trained in the 1950s, I was denied, along with a generation of my peers in the design disciplines, an integrated view of architectural history because our professors, including Gropius and Giedion and their followers, did not present the full historic information that they themselves had been given by their teachers, and thus did not grant us the opportunity to make our own ideological choices. I have, therefore, not had the historic perspective that the educated professional of a hundred years ago might reasonably expect. For instance, Corbusian ideas, such as a building's expression generating from the inside, from its own plan or functional diagram, or his ideas about the architectural object in space were not open to question, no matter how obviously limited they may have been. Until recently little debate or theoretical refinement had occurred in modernism, leaving the legitimate ideas of modernism unseparated from those that perhaps should have been discarded. Most criticism related to modernism has come in the form of denunciation from postmodernists.

Abstraction had removed most of the expressive content and narrative from modernist design, and references to nature were generally missing from "internationalist" thinking. Social, democratic, or economic purpose had largely replaced metaphor, though how a dialogue with the users would be achieved was not clear. Without this dialogue, or even an agreed-upon language, what "democratic design" might mean is a question whose answer still escapes me.

My own work started out as an exploration of two major themes. First was the extension of the building form to create a setting (read *pedestal*) for the precious object, the building. The second theme was the transition from this setting to the surrounding existing landscape.

As a modernist, by the early 1970s, I gradually became concerned at the increasingly picturesque tendencies in my own work, which was in sharp contrast to the minimal artwork of the 1960s that I had been at this same time privately collecting. These artworks seemed to me to reflect and extend the work of my heroes, the early modernist architects, especially Mies van der Rohe, Louis Kahn, and the Los Angeles case study architects of the 1950s.

The 1960s work of the artists Frank Stella, Carl Andre, Sol LeWitt, Donald Judd, Dan Flavin, Robert Morris, and others seemed to me to analytically reaffirm and revive the simplicity, formal strength, and clarity that had been the best part of my educational entrance into modernism. During these early years, though I was familiar with Corbusian comparisons between Greek temples and ocean liners, I did not relate any part of historic classicism to the enterprise of modernism. After all, history had been defined as the enemy of modernism.

In my interest in developing a classical and modern working theory of landscape architecture, both academic and experiential, I have identified two general lines of development for European landscapes throughout the classical periods. The first is the largely agricultural development of the countryside spreading out from the village and urban centers. These were the subject of writing and criticism up through the early nineteenth century of such important figures as John Loudon and Thomas Jefferson. The backgrounds in architectural and portrait paintings changed from wild nature to agriculture in the early nineteenth century. Landscape gardening was concerned with agricultural issues into the twentieth century in England and America, and these concerns included aesthetic considerations.

Donald Judd, Permanent installation of concrete works, *1981–1984. Chinati Foundation, Marfa, Texas*

The other general line of development was that of architectural extension. These outdoor spaces beginning in the fifteenth century were designed largely by architects with the help of gardeners. They generally took the form of rooms, terraces, staircases, and ornaments defined architecturally by stone and paving and by topiary treated as stone. It was not until the landscape park movement in France and England in the eighteenth century that these two lines of thought, architectural and agricultural, converged. But at this point the picturesque aspects overwhelmed the formal or geometric development of the previous three hundred years. To the uneducated eye, they represented not art but nature itself.

This pictorialism overshadowed the achievements of the great gardens of the châteaux and particularly those of Andre Le Nôtre. It has been felt that the English gardens were more an expression of modernism because they represented "nature." Frederick Law Olmsted made much of this idea and considered it therapeutic for the ills of industrial urbanism. Ian McHarg has also embraced this notion in his attack on French and Renaissance gardens. The French gardens may, however, be a more classical line of investigation as they clearly express the highest form of the agricultural progression stemming from the twelfth and thirteenth centuries. Redevelopment of the French (and later English) agricultural landscape was achieved by the management techniques of the church, in its effort to finance and build the cathedrals through husbandry of the countryside. One can clearly see in Le Nôtre's work the hedgerows, the wood lots, and the ponds of drained lowlands and the direct geometries of the French rural countryside. They are certainly as much classical expressions of nature as the more romantic pictorial gardens.

In Asia, the garden was thought of as an art form separate from architecture or agriculture, parallel in its value and autonomy with the arts of painting, sculpture, music, and poetry. A language of form and a great range of expression were formulated. The cultivation and refinement of these gardens is in many ways analogous to that of Western classical architecture.

Modernism has yet to develop an articulate body of landscape theory, though one can see in the few masterworks explorations of various formal approaches drawn from the several artistic styles or combinations of them, such as constructivism or surrealism.

With the exception of the brief French garden movement in the 1920s, neither de Stijl, the Bauhaus, nor CIAM had addressed landscape design in an essential or principal way. They generally viewed open space and nature as quantitative and "empty" space in which to set buildings, rather than as objective qualitative design acts. This open space was considered to function similarly to the white box of the modern gallery or museum, as a neutral environment. Most architects to this day have a rather romantic view of landscape as wild nature or "soft" setting. The early modernist architects were introduced to landscape design first in England and more emphatically in the United States in the late 1930s when leaders of these movements fled Germany and other parts of Europe and began to teach in American universities.

My work for the last twenty years has been an attempt to weave together the strands of classicism and European and Asian garden formalism and those of modernism, including the late modernists and midcentury minimalists, as I understand them. The result is what I consider minimalism in the landscape.

Donald Judd, Arbor. Chinati Foundation, Marfa, Texas

Minimalism in the Landscape

Distinct from the specificity of its art world argument relating to a certain group of artists at a certain moment in the 1960s, minimalism in the landscape seems to me to represent a revival of the analytic interests of the early modernists that parallel in many respects the spirit of classicism. It is the formal reinvention and the quest for primary purity and human meaning that signify its spiritual strength: an interest in mystery and nonreferential content are thereby linked to the quest of classical thought.

As with the term and idea of classicism, minimalism has entered our fast-paced society and been further defined and redefined by varying artistic and cultural disciplines. In this greater context, minimalism continues to imply an approach that rejects any attempt to intellectually, technically, or industrially overcome the forces of nature. It suggests a conceptual order and the reality of changing natural systems with geometry, narrative, rhythm, gesture, and other devices that can imbue space with a sense of unique place that lives in memory.

Despite the broader scope of my use of the term *minimalism*, a reference to a quintessential minimalist artist is illuminating. Donald Judd insisted that minimalism is first and foremost an expression of the objective, a focus on the object in itself, rather than its surrounding context or interpretation. Minimalism is not referential or representative, though some viewers will inevitably make their own historical or iconic projections. In correlation, though minimalist landscape exists in the larger context of the environment, and though it may employ strategies of interruption or interaction and one can see beyond the designed "objects" to the larger landscape, the focus is still on the designed landscape itself, its own energy and space. Scale, both in context and internally experienced, remains primarily important. And as with minimal art, minimalist landscape is not necessarily or essentially reductivist, although these works often do have minimum components and a directness that implies simplicity.

With these parameters, minimalism in landscape architecture opens a line of inquiry that can illuminate and guide us through some of the difficult transitions of our time: the simplification or loss of craft, transitions from traditional natural materials to synthetics, and extensions of human scale to the large scale, in both space and time, of our mechanically aided modern life. And minimalism in this context suggests an artistically successful approach to dealing with two of the most critical environmental problems we currently face: mounting waste and dwindling resources.

An inquiry into minimalism in the landscape now seems to be especially timely. Recent developments in landscape architecture, architecture, and urban design during what has been termed our postmodern era have questioned the legitimacy of modernist design, with some favoring a return to classicism. Much of the recent work and thought in this area has focused on formal and decorative issues on the one hand and sociological and functional issues on the other. Minimalism, one of the manifestations of the last moment of high modernism in the visual arts, has itself, of course, many compelling affinities with classicism. Rather than focusing on design and functional issues as mutually exclusive, minimalism leads to examination of the abstract and the essential, qualities of both classicist and modernist design.

It is interesting to recall that when the youthful Le Corbusier journeyed through the Middle Eastern and Mediterranean lands before World War I in 1911, he was drawn to Turkish mosques, Byzantine monasteries, and Bulgarian houses, because of certain qualities, particularly silence, light, and simple, austere form. On the Acropolis of Athens, however, he was overwhelmed and awed by the Parthenon, the "undeniable master," which he later interpreted as a distillation of form, an unexcelled product of standardization. A moment had been reached, he concluded, when nothing more could be taken away. It was a moment of perfection, a defining of the classic. It so happens that I felt a similar response to one particular Le Nôtre garden when I visited it in the 1970s. Chantilly, a great garden of stone, water, space, and light, also represents a superb example of form reduced to its essential perfection. Chantilly seemed to me then and seems to me still to share in its essence an understanding and intent that is both classic and minimal.

Carl Andre, Lead-Magnesium Plain, *1969.*
Photograph courtesy Paula Cooper Gallery, New York

These thoughts are a progress report of my personal journey as a landscape architect who came of age at the height of modernism in American environmental design. They are informed by the gardens, landscapes, designs, artists, and insights that have helped to shape my perceptions and to chart my particular course of inquiry to this point. They offer one personal approach to the making of environments that seems to be especially needed at this time in human history: environments that are serene and uncluttered, yet still expressive and meaningful. More than ever, we need to incorporate in our built environment places for gathering and congregation, *along with* spaces for discovery, repose, and privacy in our increasingly bewildering, spiritually impoverished, overstuffed and undermaintained garden Earth.

Art Is Not a Garden

My transition from art appreciator to my concern with integrating ideas about art in my landscape work was a gradual one. At first I was a collector, and I haunted galleries and read books, art magazines, and catalogues, especially about the minimalists, voraciously. I thought there was no professional intent nor crossover thinking in my interest, only the curiosity about the beauty and meaning of the art and the visual and intellectual energy it engendered.

After several years I remember noticing what I thought of as landscape ideas in the early striped paintings of Frank Stella: how the internal design of the patterns were able to define the shape of a two-dimensional painting, obviating the frame and eliminating the possibility of being read as an abstracted image. This was like a garden without walls, able to exist in a spatial context and also to be an object apart.

Then, Carl Andre's metal floor pieces began to seem to me powerful metaphors for gardens: all flat ground plane and almost no third dimension, yet completely controlling the character and nature of the "empty" space above. These reminded me of the Persian carpets of the desert bedouin: movable, ideal, and intimate gardens. One Andre work, *144 Blocks and Stones*, 1973, was especially dynamic by this reading. In its installation, all the walls (read *architecture*) of the gallery were emptied and the floor (read *landscape*) became a complex and mysterious totem or game. The materials were humble, even mundane, but the result was intensely compelling, and I experienced a strong connection between the mysterious spirits of art and gardens.

Yet another Andre work, *Secant*, 1977, was placed in an ordinary meadow. The meadow was naturally beautiful but hardly different from thousands just like it in the region. By Andre's profoundly simple placement of a series of cut timbers, the meadow was transformed into a place generating and demanding conscious and unconscious memory.

In a similar way, Christo's *Running Fence*, 1972–1976, was built in a generic landscape of hills rolling westward to the Pacific Ocean in Marin and Sonoma Counties in California, and enlivened the landscape to a condition of high celebration. I had grown up and lived most of my life in these same coastal hills and thought I knew them better than most and more than any other landscapes of my experience. Yet I had never seen them in quite this way or felt so strongly a part of them before. That a string of silken sheets could accomplish such revisioning was astounding. Still, at that moment, I could see no direct relationship between my response and excitement as a viewer and anything that I had thought of or made as a landscape architect.

Over time, many more artworks reinforced and expanded my growing sense of the potential for the integration of art and the landscape, and ultimately I found myself dissatisfied with only collecting works of art. Following a summer tour of French gardens in the late 1970s, the cohesion among the great, historic formal gardens, the art of the minimalist, and my own vision for landscape architecture crystallized, and I began to try to make gardens in a new way. The first efforts were quite tentative. It became apparent that the simple transfer of an idea inspired by work in a gallery or specific site would not in itself be a successful strategy or even a new direction of landscape architecture, given the other dimensions of nature that needed inclusion.

Though the concept of objectification was useful, for instance, the idea of manifesting meaning could not be isolated from other pressing considerations. Objects and formal systems are seen in the landscape in strong contrast to the larger environment that includes not only the particulars of a site and its surroundings but, more comprehensively, the organic rhythms of the daily movement of the sun and moon, the changes of seasonal light and climate shifts, and, especially, the extreme acts of nature and the more random characteristics of birth, growth, and decline. This complex interaction between nature and even the simplest introduced or placed object magnifies and compounds the anticipation and allowance necessary for conceiving of work on the land, making time as large a factor as place.

This realization, though new to me at the time in the magnitude of its clarity, is nevertheless really obvious. In the field of contemporary landscape design, though, the element of time and the reality of unpredictability are not often addressed in their primacy for three largely Cartesian reasons. First, a scientific/technologic tendency to want to dissect, overpower, and control, rather than to celebrate, the mystery of nature still dominates. Then, an inability or unwillingness to deal with natural complexity and change in our desire to offer "expert" service remains. (Predictability occupies perhaps too high a place in our value system.) And third, there is an overemphasis on detail and specific program stemming from a questionable acceptance of modernist architectural thought.

If "form follows function," then analyzing function to make form follow it becomes the priority. Form then merely expresses or reveals function above any other, higher ideal as a measure of

Carl Andre, Secant, Roslyn, New York, 1977. Photograph courtesy Paula Cooper Gallery, New York

satisfaction of design goals. The more intuitive, artistic approach to designing in and with nature and, initially, the more generalized and universalized plan reveal the wonderful properties and prospects of interaction between a human physical act and the ever changing world of open space.

The real problem with my conceptual and actual consideration of landscape architecture, then, was that there was an abundance of core ideas available but the parameters of choosing ones that would resonate in a useful, meaningful, beautiful, and even mysterious or spiritual way were as yet undetermined.

The unlikely combination of the thought and art of the minimalists and the conditions of natural open space, unrealized by contemporary landscape designers, opened up an intriguing and challenging path of investigation and experimentation. In this way of looking at the problem, dealing with all aspects of the public realm (including derelict land, streets, parking lots, and rooftops, as well as more traditional pursuits with gardens, parks, and plazas) is a revelation. It offers a basis of reviewing our cities and suburbs, old and new.

Visibility

To be visible, I believe an object must be seen, at least partly, in and for itself. If it is largely subordinated to context or if it is confused with some existing form of the environment, the work is drained of its ability to be expressive, to carry meaning or narrative or to imprint on the memory. Even high decoration cannot gain conscious attention if it cannot achieve objecthood alongside the other existing artistic presences.

Modern society is fragmented and commercial. The landscape is seen as open and empty and much of modern urban space is left over, on the edge, neglected. Symbols of commemoration have declined. Natural, historic, and remote images are fast replacing real outdoor experience. So what are the possible strategies for visibility within these conditions?

Fragmentation, both physical and experiential, tends to break down one's sense of natural order. Streams are interrupted and put in pipes; hills and mountains are cut, removed or visually scarred. Pedestrian ways are rendered discontinuous. Buildings and chemical pollution block natural lines of sight to the major defining landforms, including the sea and even the sky. Natural distinguishing landscape units such as the Los Angeles Basin, the island of Manhattan, the Charles River in Boston, and a myriad of other examples, have been visually weakened by man-made roads, highways, buildings, and, in some cases, man-made landscapes as well.

Underlying these mutations are a diminished sense of order, quiet, and visual dimension and the loss of the stability that premodern humans found in mountains, plains, lakes, rivers, and seas, agrarian developments, villages, and small city settlements. In all of these situations, spatial orderings referenced a larger nature that replicated a relationship to the earth as a whole.

If simple order itself strongly contrasts fragmentation, marginalization, and discontinuity, then the values of reduction and focus offer a direction for our culture. Ordering devices common to much minimal art and to traditional formal gardens include seriality and repetition, geometry (particularly linear and point grids), perceived extension of dimensions, linear gesture, and visual exploitation of edges and centers, including bilateral and asymmetrical symmetry. The exploration of texture and pattern, scale and color contrast, as well as synthetic versus natural, living versus inert, are also avenues to order in this context. To this list can be added commemoration, narrative, and symbol. Ultimately, in the necessity to return analysis to essential visual properties, the goal is to achieve mystery rather than irony.

Landscape as Art

Open space is equally important, or perhaps even more crucial, to civic, cultural, and modern social life than interior space. The designed landscape can be as capable of commemorative expression or mystery as any facade or other architectural form or dimension. It is the public open space formed for function only, filled with purposeful but artistically bereft roads, parking, and service spaces, for instance, that carries the message of indifferent ugliness, thereby tarnishing the hopes of modernism to the degree that modernism is felt to have in fact failed. A large part of that failure lies in site planning and open space areas, the public realm of cities and towns.

One of the themes of classical architecture is the referencing back to nature and the search for the classical ideal through generations of invention, reinterpretation, and expression and the interweaving of these themes with those of an ever expanding and enriched culture. How then can one conceive of a parallel within an artform that is in itself in large part nature? I think the answer may lie in the ability to look at nature in two ways, both wild and tame.

Wild nature and open landscape are never in a state of stability or permanence as is the state implied by classical architecture. Therefore, architecture is probably a poor analogy for landscape. Music, though often used to describe landscape, is too ephemeral, and though one can describe space with music (for example, the work of John Cage), it is not physically habitable as open space is. Open space is a very complex medium to influence, subject as it is to the constant multiple changes of daily, seasonal, and maturing cycles and complicated by sound, odor, temperature, and precipitation. Of all the arts, it most nearly compares with the complexity of human life.

A constantly changing nature defines a distinct artform, unique to itself and separate from the others. Existing criteria are still in the state of creation, still open to development, expansion, dialogue, possibility, direction, and hope.

There are many questions to consider: Is it too wild? Can the modern landscape (natural or urban) really be controlled sufficiently to be context and content for an artform? Can a conception of the landscape bring enough control within the complexity of modern existence? In other words, can the means we have achieve the ends we seek? I feel that they can and that signposts to that success lie in the innovative works of Luis Barragan, Isamu Noguchi, Roberto Burle Marx, Dan Kiley, Lawrence Halprin, and the other great landscape designers of our time. For me, minimalism is one line of inquiry that directs us to the breadth of solutions that our culture awaits.

Richard Long, Sea Lava Circles, *1988.*
Chinati Foundation, Marfa, Texas

IBM Solana, Westlake and Southlake, Texas

Minimalist Gardens: Portfolio

Marlborough Street Roof Garden

Necco Garden

Cambridge Center Roof Garden

Burnett Park

Tanner Fountain

IBM Clearlake

Marlborough Street Roof Garden

Necco Garden

Burnett Park

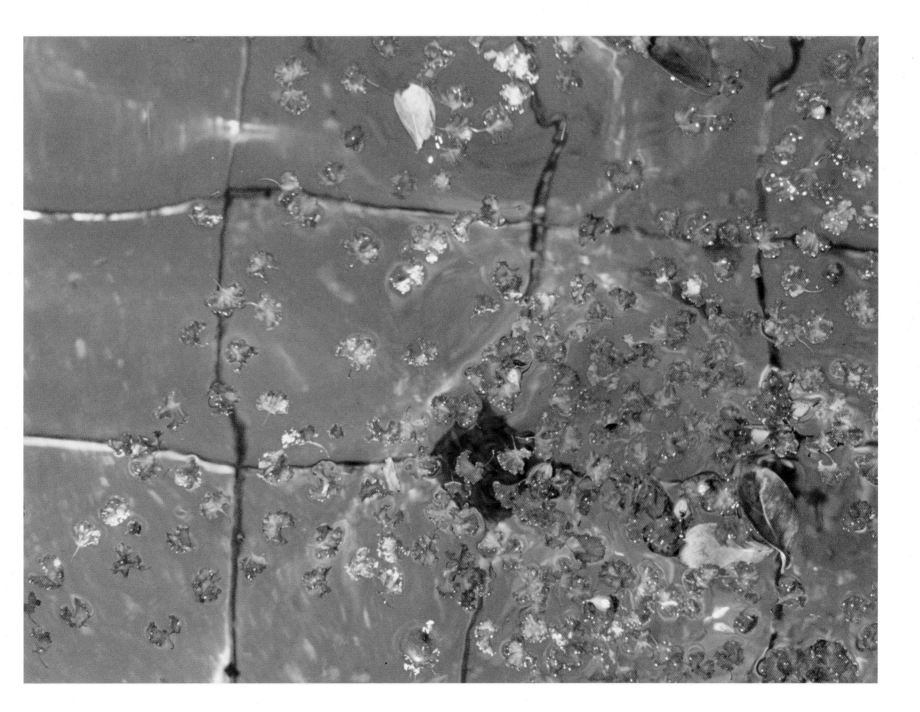

Burnett Park

Tanner Fountain

Tanner Fountain

Tanner Fountain

IBM Clearlake

IBM Clearlake

IBM Solana

Institute for Advanced Biomedical Research

Herman Miller, Inc.

IBM Solana

IBM Solana

IBM Solana

Institute for Advanced
Biomedical Research

Herman Miller, Inc.

Herman Miller, Inc.

Ayala Triangle

Plaza Tower and Town Center Park

IBM Japan Makuhari Building

Hotel Kempinski

Ayala Triangle

Plaza Tower and Town Center Park

IBM Japan Makuhari Building

IBM Japan Makuhari Building

Hotel Kempinski

Hotel Kempinski

Hotel Kempinski

Marugame Station Plaza

Europa-Haus

University of California at San Diego Library Walk

Marugame Station Plaza

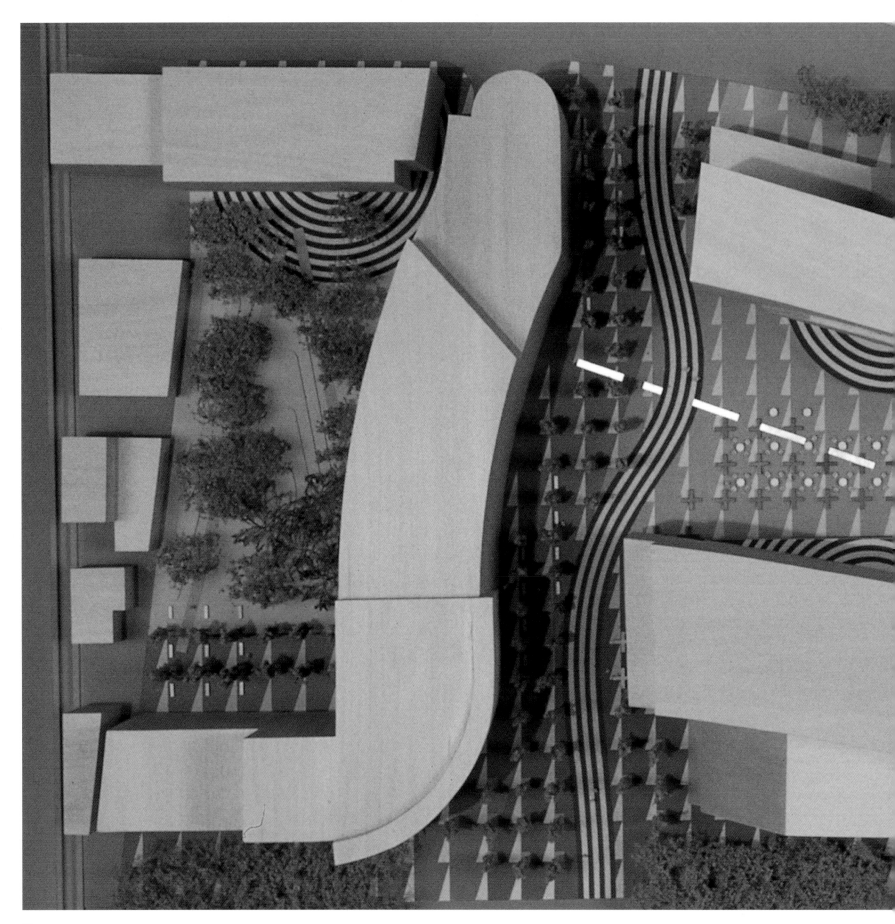

University of California at San Diego Library Walk

Toyota Municipal Museum of Art

Harima Science Garden City

Center for the Advanced Science and Technology

Toyota Municipal Museum of Art

Toyota Municipal Museum of Art

Toyota Municipal Museum of Art

Harima Science Garden City

Center for the Advanced Science and Technology

21st Century Tower and Plaza

Oyama Training Center

Sony Center Berlin

Saitama Sky Forest Plaza

21st Century Tower and Plaza

Oyama Training Center

Sony Center Berlin

Saitama Sky Forest Plaza

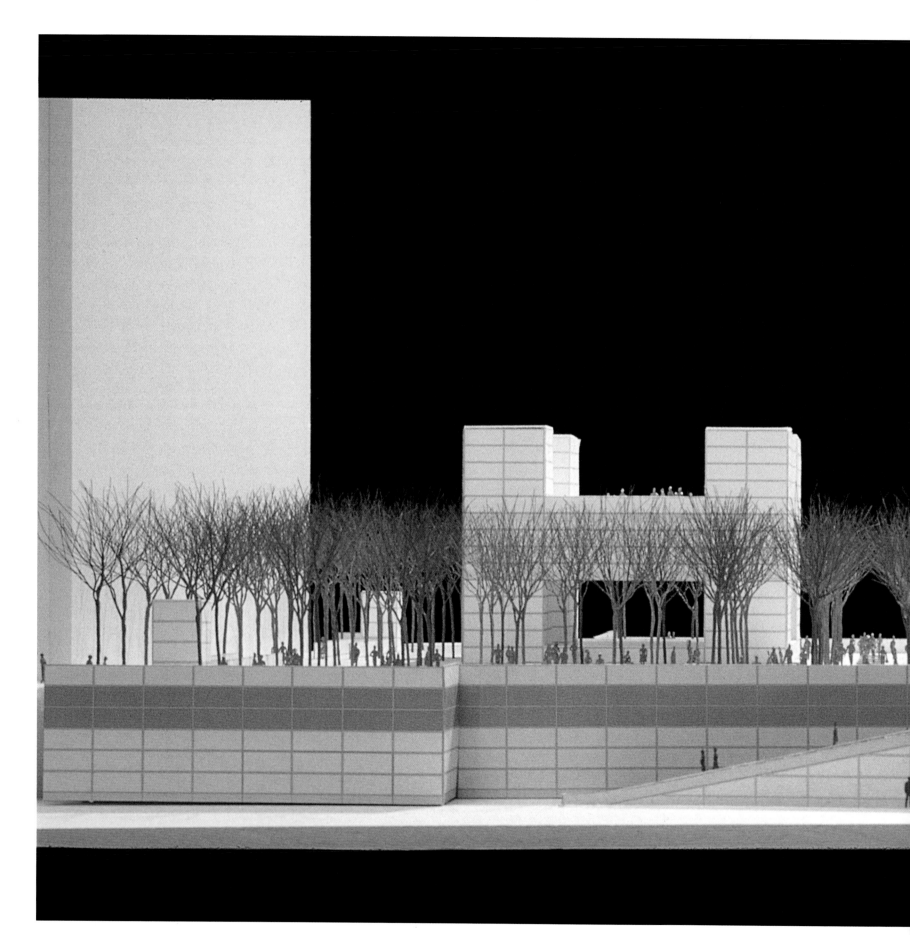

Within the image: Security, Parking, Parking, Ingress

Saitama Sky Forest Plaza

Garden Descriptions

Marlborough Street Roof Garden

Location: Boston, Massachusetts
Landscape
Architect: Peter Walker and
Martha Schwartz
with John Wong
Completed: 1979

With the 190 Marlborough Street Roof Garden in 1979, Peter Walker and Martha Schwartz created an installation garden joining, almost parodying, classic Le Nôtre formalism with contemporary materials and effect. With the three distinct components of a field of empty flower pots of illusory scale placed in a regular pattern, a sky-reflecting mirrored parterre positioned on colored gravel, and a "living" area carpeted with Astroturf, the roof garden creates a new space among the rooftops of old Boston. Whitewashed skylights serve as nighttime colored light beacons. The pop-surrealism of this garden, incorporating a seriality characteristic of minimalism, expresses the expanded possibilities of garden making.

Necco Garden

Location: Cambridge, Massachusetts;
temporary installation at
the Massachusetts Institute
of Technology
Landscape
Architect: Peter Walker and
Martha Schwartz
Temporarily
installed: 1980

Commissioned by the campus art gallery to create a temporary garden installation as part of May Day festivities at the Massachusetts Institute of Technology, Peter Walker and Martha Schwartz selected local and seemingly mundane materials to create a parterre of pastel-colored Necco candy wafers and tires painted with pastel colors. On a 350-by-550-foot lawn, the team invented two grids overlaid at different angles. The ironic formality of the project defied many viewers' concepts of what constitutes art or a garden. This investigation blurs the distinctions between art making and garden making, between the conventional and innovative in marking the land.

Mirror parterre, proportioned to Back Bay windows

Entry stair with Astroturf

Garden in "Great Space" with view toward the Charles River

Astroturf "lawns"

Skylights as lanterns illuminated from below

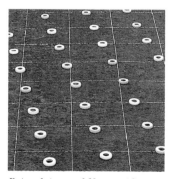

Painted tires and Necco grids

Cambridge Center
Roof Garden

Location: *Cambridge, Massachusetts*
Architect: *Moshe Safdie and Associates*
Landscape
Architect: *Peter Walker with*
        The SWA Group
Completed: *1979*

Cambridge Center Roof Garden is an orchestration of various experiments with the interweaving of plane and pattern, generated by artistic interest and enhanced by the technical necessity of using only lightweight materials. On the rooftop of a parking structure, Walker created a surreal parterre on a ground of purple-gray gravel. An area of sky-blue concrete diamonds carpets one major segment, while low, angled hedges assembled like systemic mazes cover the other important section. Cubist white sculptural structures made of metal piping populate the garden as trellises or trees would, serving to further activate the dynamic energy of the parterre with their vertical form and intricate, self-contained interiors.

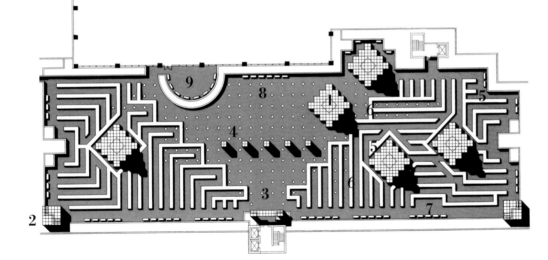

1 Trellis
2 Gazebo
3 Arch
4 Columns
5 Vine planter
6 Shrub planter
7 Crushed stone
8 Concrete plates
9 Cafe terrace

0   60 feet

Juniper and gravel "maze"

Gravel, concrete squares, and metal "trees"

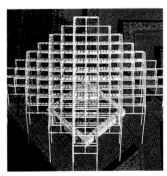

Structured "trees" seen from above

Burnett Park

Location: *Fort Worth, Texas*
Client: *Charles Tandy Foundation*
Landscape
Architect: *Peter Walker with The SWA Group*
Completed: *1983*

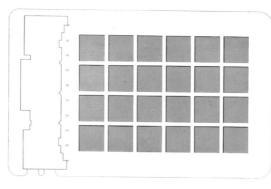

Orthogonal grid

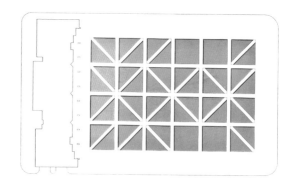

Partial diagonal grid

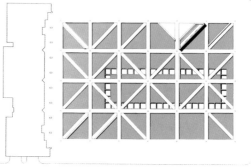

Lowered pool layer

Entrance with Matisse wall and diagonal bench walls

1 Stone walk
2 Pools
3 Matisse "Backs"
4 Shrub planters
5 Tower
6 Lowered grass
7 Plaza

0 ———— 75 feet

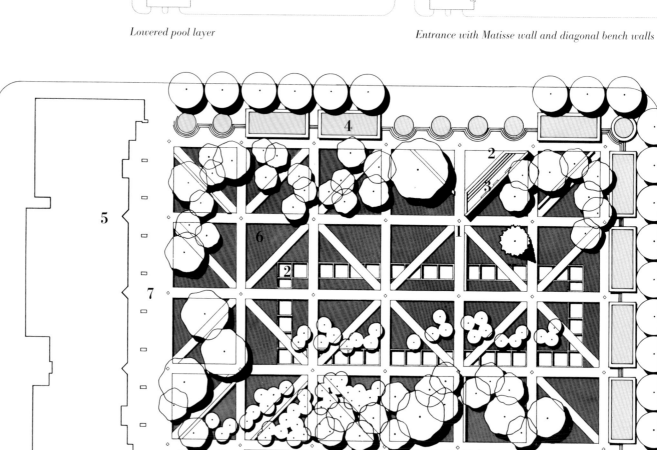

Peter Walker's use of the grid sometimes advances seemingly opposing views and purposes. Like the use of the grid in the early work of such minimalist artists as Robert Smithson, Robert Morris, Michael Heizer, and, most distinctively, Sol LeWitt, Walker employs a grid to manifest the detached regularity of industrial systems and to define a flat plane or dimensional form. Other twentieth-century artists, especially painters such as Piet Mondrian, Josef Albers, Ad Reinhardt, and Agnes Martin, have selected the grid as a vehicle for intimation of the sublime, and this orderly manifestation of beauty and cosmic pattern is also apparent in much of Walker's work. As a strictly pragmatic function, the grid is also a vehicle for organizing visual ideas, especially those relating to space.

In 1983, when asked to rehabilitate a park in Fort Worth, Texas, that was originally designed more than sixty years before, Peter Walker approached the faceted project with a literal, multidimensional plan. Burnett Park was to serve the community in several ways. As a park in the conventional sense of a green place to find natural space in which to relax and contemplate, Walker designed a space with grass, trees, and a pool of water, and places to sit, lie down, and play. As a public and urban plaza, it required solid gathering spaces, pedestrian walkways, effective night lighting, and the presence and distinction to serve as the gateway to the downtown area.

Conceived in three horizontal geometric layers, the top layer of Burnett Park is composed of a raised dual system of orthogonal and diagonal gridded pathways made from pink carnelian granite. These draw a web on the surface of the park, casting shadows on the sections of green lawn, the layer just below the linear patterns of granite. The sunken lawn provides the grounding of the field and yet interacts vibrantly with the shifting patterns of the intersecting granite. The contrast of hard and soft, cool and lush, formal and vernacular, is further emphasized by the third and deepest layer, constructed from a series of square pools placed consecutively to create a rectangle. This form is contiguous to segments of both the grass and the granite, offering counterpoints to one's perception of the multilayered composition.

The park is illuminated by squares of light interspersed within the granite pathways, fixtures in the trees and a series of five-foot-tall water wands placed within the rectangular pool. These function as miniature fountains and, with their fiber-optic lighting elements, as candlelight points.

The care and intricacies of Burnett Park's design create a new awareness of space and function. Although providing the individual details required of a park and a plaza, it does so in a way that communicates beyond the everyday experience. The park seems to mandate a consciousness of the ways in which it divides and uses space differently, heightening the awareness of the people who use it. These evoked responses may not always be soothing or familiar, but do offer a change and challenge to society, constituting an informing and uplifting experience.

Park seen from above

Pool with fountain

Fiber-optic lights in steel wands

Cut stone orthogonal and diagonal grids

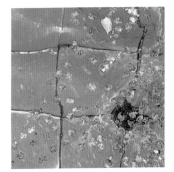

Pool with mirror tile lining

Tanner Fountain

Location: Cambridge, Massachusetts
Client: Harvard University
Landscape
Architect: Peter Walker with The SWA Group
Fountain
Consultant: Richard Chaix
Steam Artist: Joan Brigham
Completed: 1984

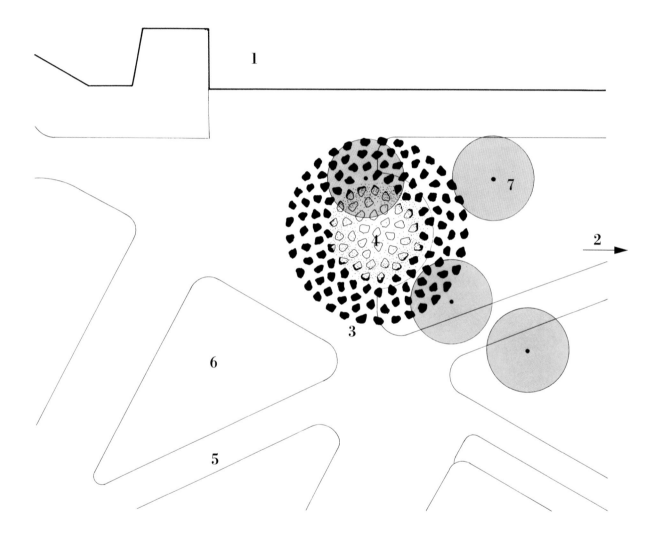

View from Harvard Yard

1 Science Center
2 Memorial Hall
3 Boulders
4 Mist fountain
5 Asphalt paths
6 Lawn
7 Trees

0   50 feet

With roots in the 2000-B.C. standing stones of Avebury and Stonehenge in England and impulses as familiar as those of a child's to pile rocks, Peter Walker has pursued marking the land with rocks and stones, eliciting private experiences in public places. Relating to the poetic objects of contemplation in Zen gardens as much as to the phenomenological systems explicit in twentieth-century minimalism and earth art, Walker uses rocks and stones to mingle symbolic references with pragmatic functionality.

Tanner Fountain at Harvard University in Cambridge, Massachusetts, is an important demonstration of Walker's affinity with the power of stones. Sited in a pedestrian crossroads surrounded by buildings, structures, and fences, Tanner Fountain is composed of a 60-foot-diameter circle, delineated by 159 stones placed in concentric but irregular circles, creating an open geometric form. Each boulder is about 4 feet by 2 feet by 2 feet, and all are embedded in the ground. Grass, asphalt, and concrete paths intersect at different points in or near the circle, varying the textures and colors of the field.

Unlike a traditional fountain, Tanner Fountain's water is generated from thirty-two nozzles located in the center of the stone area, emitting a mist in the spring, summer, and fall seasons that hovers like a cloud. The mist is refracted by daylight, producing rainbows. In the evening, lights charge the mist and the space with a mysterious glow, reflecting the light from below. In winter, when the mist would freeze, the stones are shrouded with steam, which then drifts off into the cold night air.

Designed as a place to stop and sit, as a gathering spot, and as a place for children to explore, as well as a point of attention for pedestrians moving in and around it, Tanner Fountain is specifically intended to be inhabited. It has also become a place to be outside, to connect with the earth, a nexus evocative of the primitive and the poetic. As an icon of mystery, the positioned stones, shimmering mists, refracted and enigmatic light, emerging and concealed shapes, all effect the sense of a living, powerful place.

Each season performs its own interpretation and transformation of Tanner Fountain, making the fountain a vehicle for observing nature and honoring the earth's cycles. Spring and summer provide clear air, lighted evenings, and green beds; autumn covers the floor of the field with richly colored leaves and makes winds that rouse the mist, providing a hearth. Winter snows blanket the rocks, revealing a sacredness to the silent mounds.

Stone circle and mist seen from above

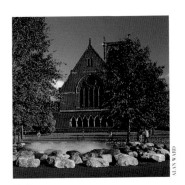

Fall

Summer

Rainbow in mist

Night lighting

Steam fountain in winter

Winter

IBM Clearlake

Location: *Houston, Texas*
Client: *IBM Corporation*
Architect: *CRSS*
Landscape
Architect: *The Office of Peter Walker and Martha Schwartz*
Completed: *1987*

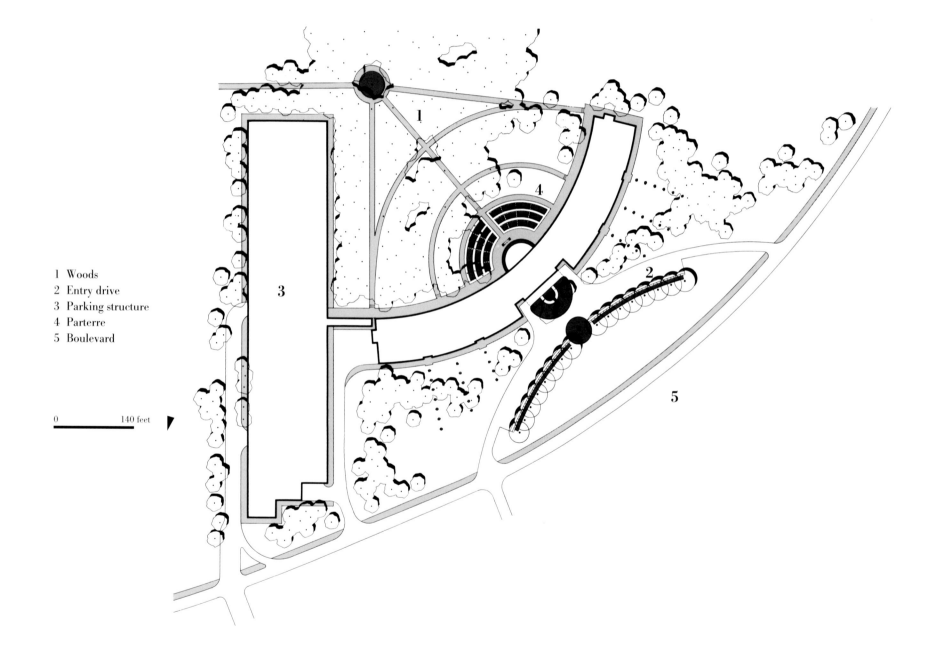

1 Woods
2 Entry drive
3 Parking structure
4 Parterre
5 Boulevard

0   140 feet

The IBM Clearlake building in Texas, designed by architects CRSS, offered the challenge of making connections and providing context for a curved, reflective glass-and-stone building sited in a swampy, wooded landscape. Based on a plan of mirroring the crescent shape of the building with a geometric central axis and concentric paths, the design radiates out from the building into an existing grove of pines.

Explicit and repeated curving segments of the garden, composed of both grass and waterlily ponds, echo the structure's form and motif, while providing their own internal focus in the overlaying of patterns. Stepping-stones are used to form broken lines that move through the pattern, unifying the diverse elements while also adding to the effect of vibrant dots made by the small shapes of the floating lily pads.

Striped reflections of both building and parterre

Radiating reflections of the sky

Geometric gravel path with random trees

Pervious path in woods

Water, grass, and gravel parterre

Radiating geometry beneath the wood

Stone gesture

IBM Solana

Location: Westlake and Southlake, Texas
Client: IBM Corporation and Maguire/Thomas Partnership

Architect: *Ricardo Legorreta Arquitectos*
Mitchell/Giurgola Architects
Leason Pomeroy and Associates
Planner: *Barton Myers and Associates*
Engineer: *Carter and Burgess, Inc.*
Landscape Architect: *Peter Walker and Partners*
(Prior to 1990, The Office of Peter Walker and Martha Schwartz)
Completed: *1991*

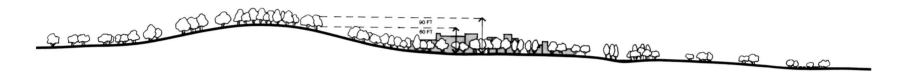

Pasture   Upper ridge   IBM buildings   Stream   Pasture   Route 114

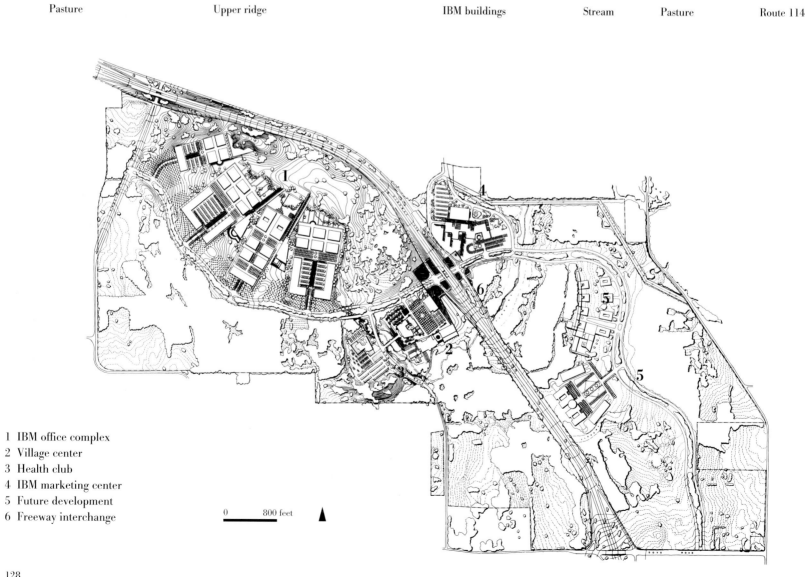

1 IBM office complex
2 Village center
3 Health club
4 IBM marketing center
5 Future development
6 Freeway interchange

0   800 feet

Solana, Spanish for "place in the sun," is an unusual example of extensive development created according to the dictates of an existing and fragile landscape. The concept for Solana mandated that the natural setting itself provide the basis for the design. Located in West Central Texas, the 850-acre site houses a series of office buildings, a villagelike shopping area, a hotel, and a myriad of open spaces including meadows, fields, grasslands, prairies, and wooded areas.

The planning of Solana sought inspiration from historic models of collaborative and often anonymous teams. Eschewing the more modern idea of a master creating heroic and individually identifiable work, Solana was perceived by the team participants, including architect Barton Myers, Mitchell/Giurgola Architects, Ricardo Legorreta Arquitectos,

and Peter Walker and Partners, as an opportunity to make their work truly site-specific and interrelated. Along with the ecological, geological, and hydrological dictates of the land, and the use requirements represented by the joint venture clients IBM Corporation and Maguire/Thomas Partnership, the team considered the scope of each others' visions and creative vocabularies to formulate an innovative and responsive approach.

One initial decision was to focus on the horizontal lines and views of the prairie, thereby establishing a model of relatively low buildings. To maintain the openness of the land, buildings were clustered together to leave unhindered spaces and acreage, relating to the cultural context of the traditional southwestern hacienda. Tackling the functional

features of the project in an effort to elevate the daily experience beyond the mundane, the team designed the highway exit ramp, creating sculptural entry gardens. Sight lines, directed out to the surrounding prairies and woods replanted with wildflowers and new oak, are lined with portals and allées of trees and canals. Noticing and exploring the horizontal perspective are encouraged by calculated placement of benches and other locations for viewing.

In contrast to the expansiveness of the overall design, more intimate and formal gardens are sited in the interior courtyards and parterres of the buildings. These are conceived and designed in direct response to the forms, colors and spirit of the architecture. Plotted rows and circles of willows and cottonwood, canals running through portals and walls,

a low fountain of stacked flagstone emanating steamy mist, black and white stone sculpted circles marking an entryway, long stacks of flagstone suggesting linear sculpture and used as benches are all placed to relate to the ultimate context. Walker and his collaborators have created an arena for the breadth of their visual ideas and interrelated them to the other elements and the overall matrix of the environment.

One of the great successes of Solana, a fine example of the best of Walker's collaborative projects, is the demonstration of his ability to communicate with and within a site, to subordinate the distinctness of his own strokes to achieve an integration and a synthesis of ideas and actual results, allowing his work to resonate with an ultimate and unifying clarity.

Geometric parterre with winding stream

Walk, allée, and canal cross parterre

Axis toward Conference Center

Axis toward the renewed pasture

Parterre with view of pasture beyond

Entry road with stone circles

Winter

Willows on canal

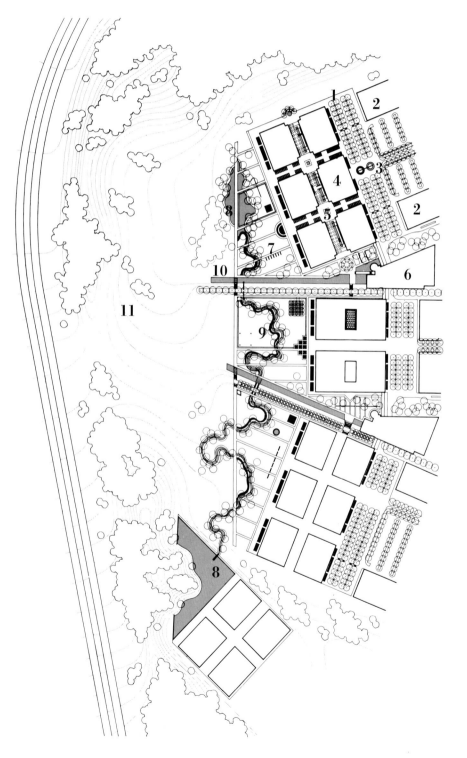

Hotel with replanted pasture

Village center

IBM office complex

1 Visitor parking
2 Parking structure
3 Entry fountains
4 Office buildings
5 Street gardens
6 Cafeteria, conference rooms
7 Parterre gardens
8 Lakes
9 Stream
10 Canal
11 Pasture

0   300 feet

Stone fountain

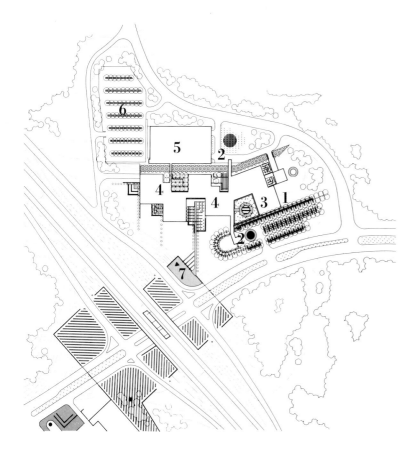

IBM marketing center

1 Visitor parking
2 Entry drop-off
3 Entry court
4 Courtyards
5 Parking structure
6 Surface parking
7 Intersection fountain

0   400 feet   ▲

Summer

Village center

Winter

1 Entry landscape
2 Office buildings
3 Village commercial center
4 Health club
5 Hotel
6 Motor court fountain
7 Freeway interchange

0   400 feet   ▲

Stone and poplar garden

Institute for Advanced Biomedical Research

Location: Portland, Oregon
Client: Oregon Health Sciences University
Architect: Zimmer Gunsul Frasca Partnership
Landscape
Architect: Peter Walker with The SWA Group
Completed: 1984

1 Beer garden cafe
2 Stepped sitting terrace
3 Stair
4 Plaza
5 Roof gardens

0   30 feet

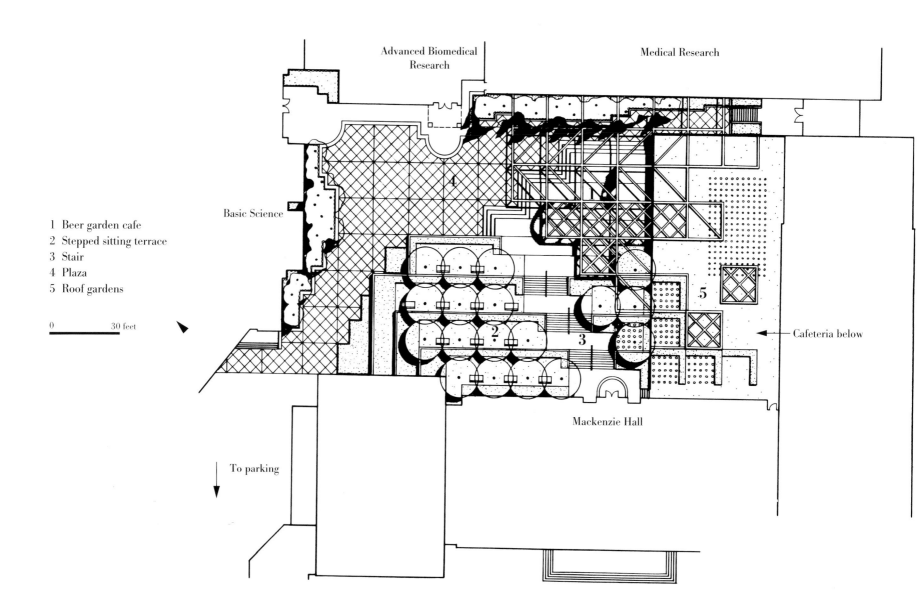

Creating a meeting place and courtyard garden that conveys both humor and restfulness, the public space for Zimmer Gunsul Frasca Partnership's Institute for Advanced Biomedical Research required innovative design for a compressed, previously gaunt space. The intent of Peter Walker was to provide a casual yet activated space, using diverse and inventively combined materials, colors, and forms.

Three essential components distinguish the space. The first is a central plaza marked by concrete paving with two superimposed grids running diagonally and squared. The pattern of these, accentuated by lines of fine moss, is echoed in other varied patterns of planters and tile bands.

A hillside garden of planted terraces provides cloisterlike settings for individual conversations and visual interaction with the other areas of the design. These intimate and distinct spots are defined with plum trees, wooden benches, and patterned retaining walls that serve as private garden walls. Small rock gardens of regularly placed violet stones add to the sense of both order and fantasy.

An elevated cafe terrace, bordered by a dynamic chevron pattern of steps, is defined with a whimsically structured pergola. This play house facade serves as shelter and as the canvas for a lattice trellis, arches, and geometrically shaped windows. The dichotomy of an open shelter shaped as a house invites an ambiguous relationship among the "interior" spaces, the people who inhabit them, and the overall spirit of the open space in which all elements interrelate.

The gardens of the Institute for Advanced Biomedical Research offer a collection of visions and spaces, creating both integration and privacy as they transform a small physical space into an expansive celebration of fresh air.

Existing condition before construction

View of plaza and stair

Stair to administration building

Stepped cul-de-sac sitting terrace

Cafe pergola

Cafe at night

Herman Miller, Inc.

Location: *Rockland, California*
Client: *Herman Miller, Inc.*
Architect: *Frank O. Gehry and Associates*
Dreyfuss and Blackford
Stanley Tigerman
Landscape
Architect: *The Office of Peter Walker and Martha Schwartz*
Completed: *1985*

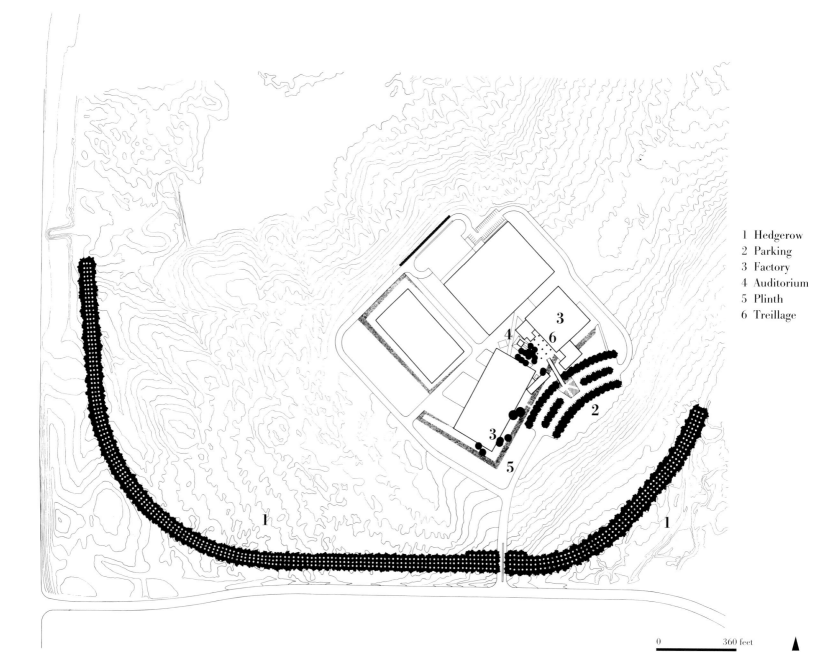

1 Hedgerow
2 Parking
3 Factory
4 Auditorium
5 Plinth
6 Treillage

0   360 feet

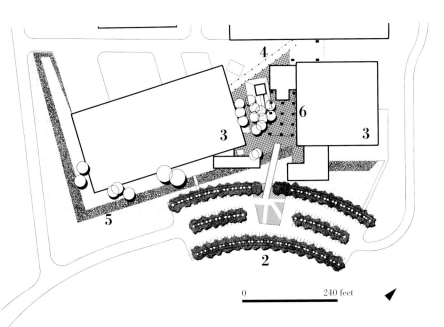

The work for Herman Miller, Inc., represents a formal approach to a situation reflecting corporate intent, distinct architecture, and a unifying and definitive landscape. It was the task of the landscape design to map an overall vista for the site, connect the building to the land, and utilize the manifest limitations and strengths to inspired ends.

The main building for Herman Miller, Inc., in Rockland, California, was designed by architect Frank Gehry as a long and low monolith sheathed in galvanized sheet metal with the treillage in copper sheeting. Constructed on a great rocky ridge, the cool modernist form of the building is belied by the warmth and richness of its surface. Peter Walker's response to the architecture and the site was to focus on the distinctive and contrasting elements of each. To accentuate the sparse and rocky characteristics of the land, Walker covered the ground with grasses and wildflowers, scattering rocks and boulders as if the ground had been showered upon in some exotic storm of raining stones.

Around the actual building, a pedestal of broken rocks (riprap) frames the structure, creating a purposeful installation of intense, small, shaped strokes of rich, polychromatic gray. A passage integrating the field and the stones is created by a patterned zone of native boulders and Chinese elm trees. These distinct components are in dialogue, each a visual narrative, as if in testimony to a surrealist happenstance on a remote piece of land.

Stony ridge with miniature wildflowers

Asphalt paving, riprap plinth, and metal buildings

Stone plinth and metal siding

Stone-lined path

Stones define parking and protect trees

Ayala Triangle

Location: Makati District,
Manila, Philippines
Client: Ayala Land, Inc.
Architect: Skidmore, Owings & Merrill, Architects
Leandro V. Locsin & Partners, Architects
Landscape
Architect: Peter Walker William Johnson and Partners
PDAA Partners
Phase One
completed: 1996

"Colonial" garden

1 Towers
2 Stock exchange
3 Museum
4 Palm grove
5 Jungle Garden
6 Plaza
7 "Ramblas"
8 "Colonial" garden

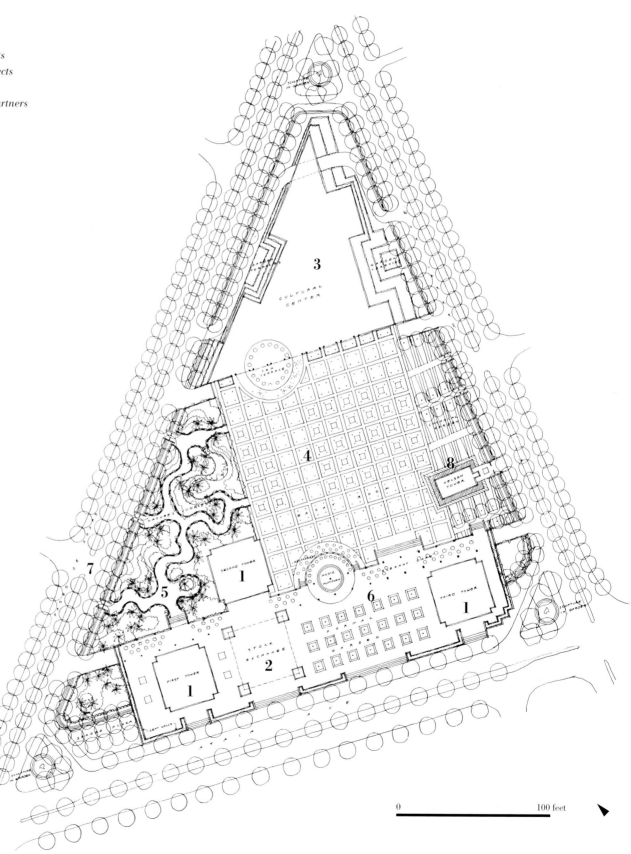

0   100 feet

The collaborative effort to realize a dynamic master plan for the Ayala Triangle, located at the heart of the financial district in Manila and retaining the form of runways of the old Manila airport, includes three sinewy high-rise office towers, a new location for the Philippine stock exchange, a major cultural center, and a large public park. Surrounding the preserved airport building is a formal bedded garden suggestive of the colonial period of Philippine history. The three streets now forming the triangle become the edge of the complex, with rain trees creating a continuous canopy over the entire street and the broad sidewalks as well. The landscape scheme offers shade and water and strong visual design to offset the extremely hot climate of the area. The core of the project, the Great Room of Palms, intended to symbolize the current democratic form of government in the Philippines, is filled with a 6-meter grid of palms, reflective pools of water, and gravel pathways.

In contrast to the regular grid of the palm grove, the Jungle Garden has irregular paths and densely planted foliage. As the more organic part of the design, it has pathways that writhe like snakes and a spacing that appears more random. This sensuously planted garden offers a welcome refuge for colorful local birds as well as for residents and visitors, creating an intimate, eccentric space characterized by the boldness of exotic flowers and fragrances.

The Great Plaza is another distinct aspect of the design, conceived as a place of arrival for the stock exchange building and the three new towers by Skidmore, Owings & Merrill, Architects. Overlooking the palm garden, it contains an outdoor restaurant and a stage for afternoon concerts.

Recognizing the colorful social and cultural community personified by the lively street life of Manila, and reminiscent of the Ramblas in Barcelona, Peter Walker has provided comfortable streetside steps for strolling and greeting along the parameters of the Ayala Triangle.

Garden   "Ramblas"   Boulevard

Section through Jungle Garden

0   50 feet

Jungle Garden

"Snake" benches

Democratic palm and pool hyperstyle garden

Sitting steps on streetside "Ramblas"

Mission Grand Axe

Location: Paris, France
Sponsor: Etablissement Public pour l'Aménagement de la Region de la Défense (EPAD)
Competition Team:
Peter Walker William Johnson and Partners
RTKL Associates, Inc.
Agence P. Lesage Associés
A.M.N.R. Architects-Urbanistes
Urban Designer:
Julia Trilling, Ph.D.
Stanford Anderson, Ph.D.
Ralph Gakenheimer, Ph.D.
Drawings: William Johnson
Competition: 1991

The grandeur of Paris lies not only in its monuments and gardens, but also in its bold network of tree-lined boulevards dominated by the east/west axis that links the Louvre, the Tuileries, the Place de la Concorde, the Champs-Élysées, and the modern business center of La Défense. In proposing to extend this axis westward for 5 kilometers, the design and planning aims of the competition submission of Peter Walker William Johnson and Partners were to restructure and revitalize the existing, fragmented elements of industry, housing, and transportation and to create a setting for social, cultural and environmental awareness.

Two main concepts to this end are the helix, which combines circular and linear motion, and the essence of the scheme, a 60-meter-wide and 5,000-meter-long meadow of grasses and wildflowers as the central gesture of the axis.

The helix image weaves throughout the plan, providing both focus on and diversion from the single, central extended line of the axis. Its sectioned geometric curve serves as a fluid catalyst while also enclosing the space contained in the arc it forms. The series of helixes presented in the design accentuates the sensuous, gliding flow of the format, interweaving direct movement with circuitous motion. A melded version of a curving

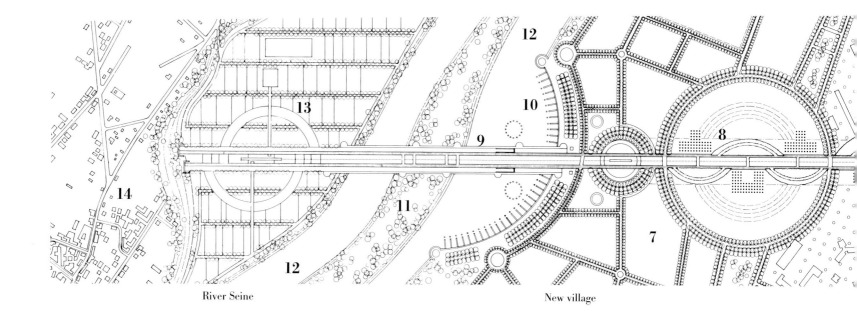

River Seine

New village

Proposed view from La Défense with the great meadow

Axis bridge at island in the Seine

Existing view from La Défense

line from the primary elements of the straight line and the circle is created. These linear arcs also make a visual connection with the complete circles contained in the design. The straight line, circle, and partial circle are rooted in human culture and in the search for spiritual connection. As the crux of a plan for the City of Paris, they create an inspiring reference.

The wildflower meadow, meant to extend the length of the axis, offers a natural and colloquial juxtaposition to the formal, geometric characteristics also within the design. Changing with the seasons, this modest and yet bold stroke supplies a contemporary commentary on the city and on the formality of great cities with monumental and historic underpinnings. Changing color and the seasonal evolutions of this meadow in the city furnish the substance and shape of the horizontal plane that runs the length of the axis. Tiny lights in the meadow glittering at night join with the starry sky to produce a mysterious fusion of spaces and moods.

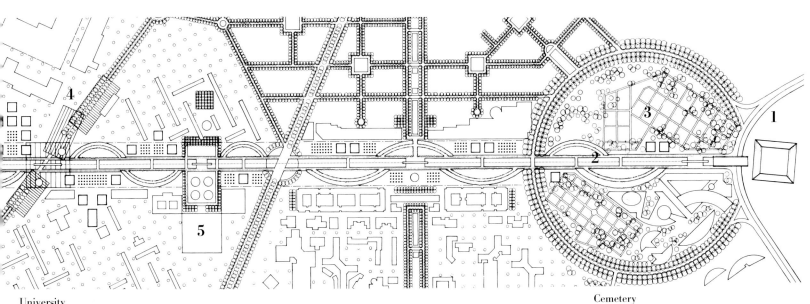

University   Cemetery

Collage plaza reunites University North and South

"Helix" bosk with cafe

View of meadow axis toward the Grand Arch

139

Plaza Tower and
Town Center Park

Location: Costa Mesa, California
Client: Anton Boulevard Associates,
             A Joint Venture of IBM Corporation
             and C. J. Segerstrom and Sons
Architect: Cesar Pelli and Associates, Design
             CRS Sirrine, Inc.
Landscape
Architect: Peter Walker and Partners
Artist: Aiko Miyawaki
Completed: 1991

1 Plaza
2 Miyawaki sculpture
3 Noguchi garden
4 Opera house plaza
5 Plaza tower
6 South Coast Plaza Hotel
7 Parking structure
8 Office
9 South Coast Reperatory Theatre
10 Restaurant
11 Orange County Performing Arts Center
12 Center tower
13 Center spa
14 Plaza theater

0   100 feet ▲

Twin pools at Plaza Tower entry

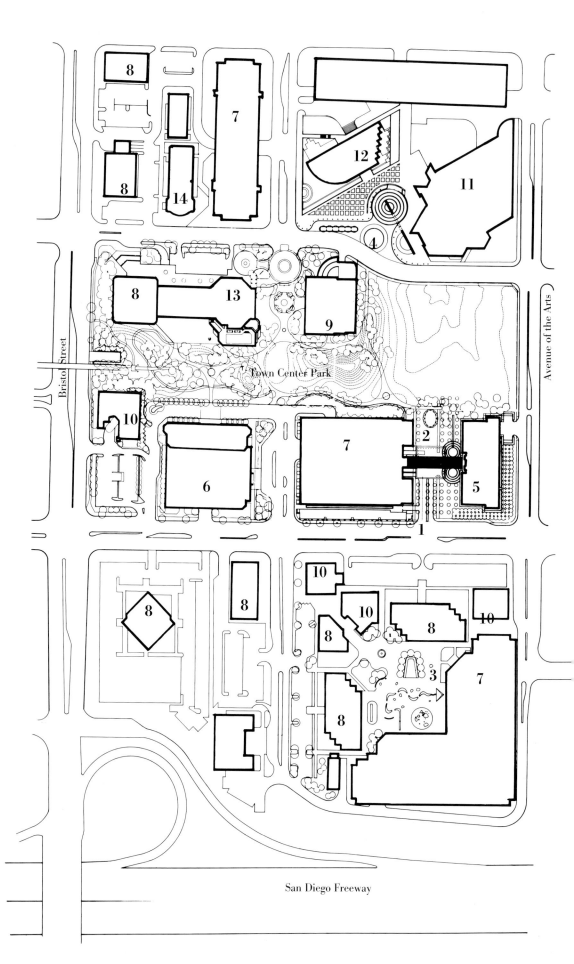

Despite the fact that the twin stainless steel pools designed by Peter Walker for the entry of Cesar Pelli's Plaza Tower serve as a remarkably successful unifying element for the building, the pedestrian and vehicular entry area, and the parking lot across the way, and are not conceived independent of these components, the pools work equally well as autonomous sculptures on the land. Incorporating grass, water, cobbles, and the stainless steel that relates to the bow-fronted Pelli structure, the reflecting water both draws and mirrors the sky as it also reacts to fluctuations of the wind and to the human touch. With boulders lining the bottom of the clear pool water, an image of both the dichotomy and integration of nature

and the urban setting continually offers its commentary. Created to mimic organic ripples from a central point while also echoing a more geometric, concentric abstraction, this simple work evolves with complexities of implication and overlay at every turn. Linear bands of stainless steel, positioned regularly within the cobblestone plaza, run between the structures and cut across the emanating, curvilinear ripples of the pools, further interrelating the various forms. Almost disguised within the public, corporate context because of the simple shapes and contextual materials, there is a clear and rich vision of beauty expressed here, confounding any preconceptions we may have about where important art is found.

The adjacent Town Center Park is enlivened by Aiko Miyawaki's *Utsurohi*, a kinetic, stainless steel sculpture composed of twelve units representing the signs of the zodiac.

Plaza Tower and Town Center Park are part of the evolving South Coast Plaza Town Center, a suburban development including commercial, recreational, and cultural activities in which Peter Walker has been involved since the early 1970s. Among the various plazas, parks, and sculpture sited throughout the Center, Isamu Noguchi's site-specific garden, *California Scenario*, is a significant and memorable lure.

View toward IBM building

Topiary and palms at opera house grand entry ramp

Miyawaki sculpture

Reflected morning light

Paving with varying degrees of reflectivity

Pool with stone lining

IBM Japan Makuhari Building

Location: Makuhari, Chiba Prefecture, Japan
Client: IBM Japan
Architect: Taniguchi and Associates
              Nihon Sekkei, Inc., Architects
Landscape
Architect: Peter Walker and Partners
Completed: 1991

1 Entry court
2 Parking
3 Pool
4 Willow island
5 Sentinel boulder
6 Cafe pavilion
7 Light line
8 Stair pavilion
9 Sky walk
10 Bamboo grove
11 Stone walls
12 Hedge
13 Grass mounds
14 Poplar grove

0   20 meters

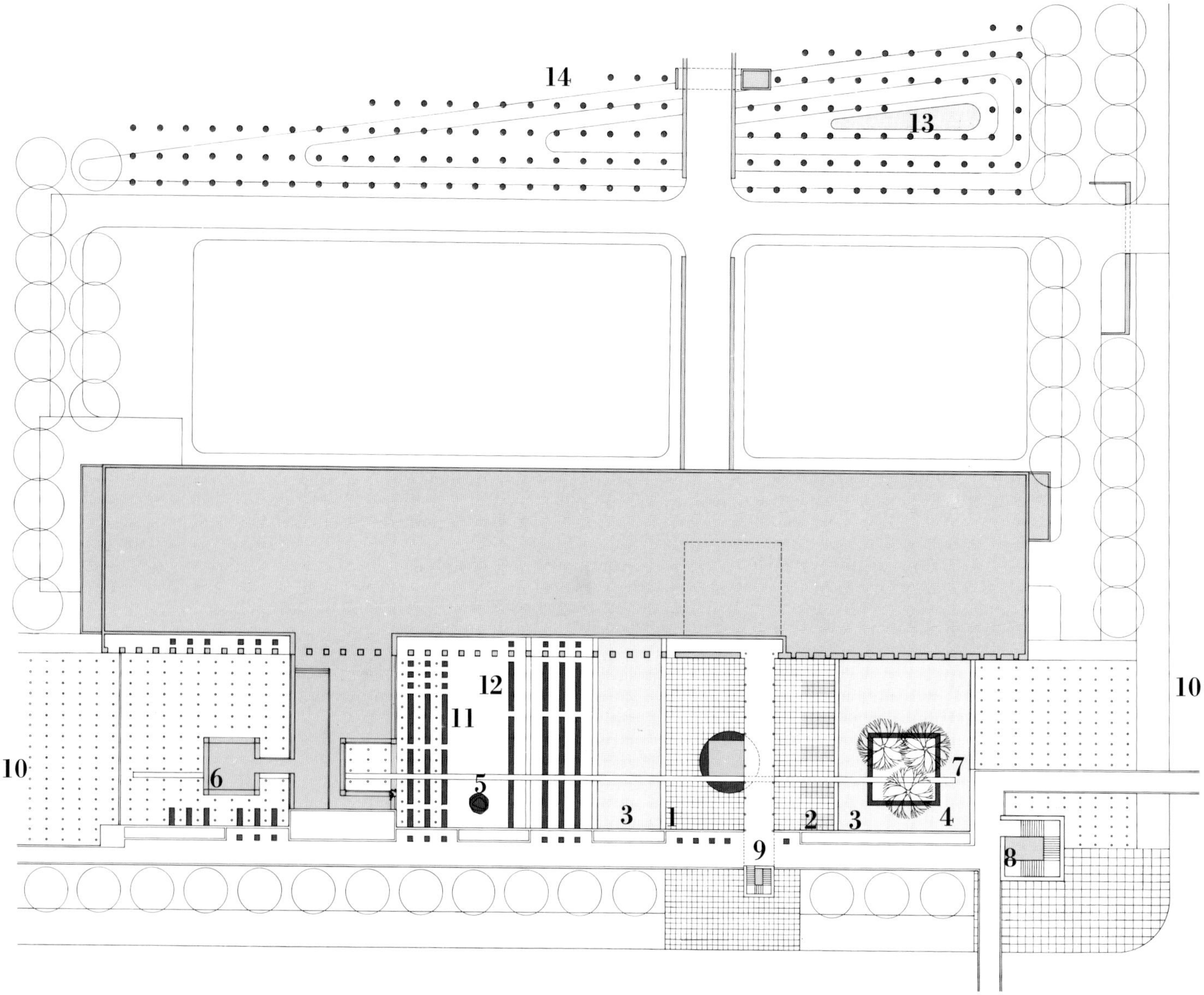

For IBM Japan's new site in Makuhari, directly outside of Tokyo, Peter Walker and Partners designed a geometrically abstract garden to be viewed as a contemplative entity from the Taniguchi and Associates eleven-story structure. The sheath of the building, composed of slabs of gray stone, functions like a traditional Japanese byobu screen, backing and framing views of the poetic garden space.

The form of the garden is inspired by Walker's idea of the early computer punch card as a metaphor for ordering the infinite possibilities in both technology and nature. It is also a literal as well as witty reference to the client, IBM. The theme of the tension among nature, art, and technology reflects a current in the vanguard of contemporary installation art, expressing a cultural idea of discord among the three disciplines. In this investigation, Walker employs one of his identifiable, even signature, stances by posing a visual resolution to the anticipated disconsonance.

IBM Makuhari uses organic and inorganic materials in components that resemble each other and can be interchangeable in the overall pattern. The garden color of varying hues and values of green is a metaphor for nature, while the organizing geometry is associated with modern systemization as well as the calm of repetitive meditation. A green slate stone is layered in bands to mirror the form of geometrically clipped hedges. Two identical pools are planted with water lilies: one in sunlight, the other in the shadow of willows. Moss and gravel areas absorb light; slate and green-tinted concrete reflect it. These contrasts and reversals reveal an ambiguity in the likeness and opposition of natural and human-made order. In the IBM garden, Walker identifies these sometimes disparate entities, ultimately providing for a unifying overlay of interrelated visual, physical, and metaphysical systems.

Reflecting on the equivalences of opposing or differing forces, the IBM garden also comments on the cultural contrasts of East and West. The garden uses materials traditional to Japanese gardens (stone, water, bamboo, willows, evergreen shrubs, moss, gravel, jade pebbles), but also employs the Western notion of the grid, incorporating hedges, stone walls, and seriality throughout.

This garden, primarily intended to be viewed rather than entered, acts as a conceptual template of a sculpture garden, with distinct segments created for unique components. Areas of hedges, a bamboo grove, the replicate pools, and a very sculptural, large, and mysteriously floating stone—each provide individual focus. Complementarily, strong integrating elements, including a glowing line of light that dissects and also joins the entire garden at ground level, the overall related geometric patterning, and a graduated green color serve to offer a total, unifying environment. It is as if Peter Walker has made a sculpture garden and filled it with a lexicon of images and artifacts of his own, much in the way that Donald Judd created architectural environments for his own sculpture.

View from above

Sun screens on sky terrace

Willow island with pebble surface

Pedestrian entry bridge over garden

Floating stone (7 x 3.5 meters)

Line of light

Lily pond penetrates building colonnade

Hotel Kempinski

Location:	*Munich Airport Center*
	Munich, Germany
Client:	*Flughafen Munchen GmbH*
Architect:	*Murphy/Jahn, Inc., Architects*
Engineer:	*Ove Arup & Partners*
Landscape	
Architect:	*Peter Walker and Partners*
Completed:	*1994*

1 Atrium
2 Entry
3 Beer garden
4 Hotel
5 Restaurant terrace
6 Parterre
7 Moving sidewalk
8 Access road

0   20 meters

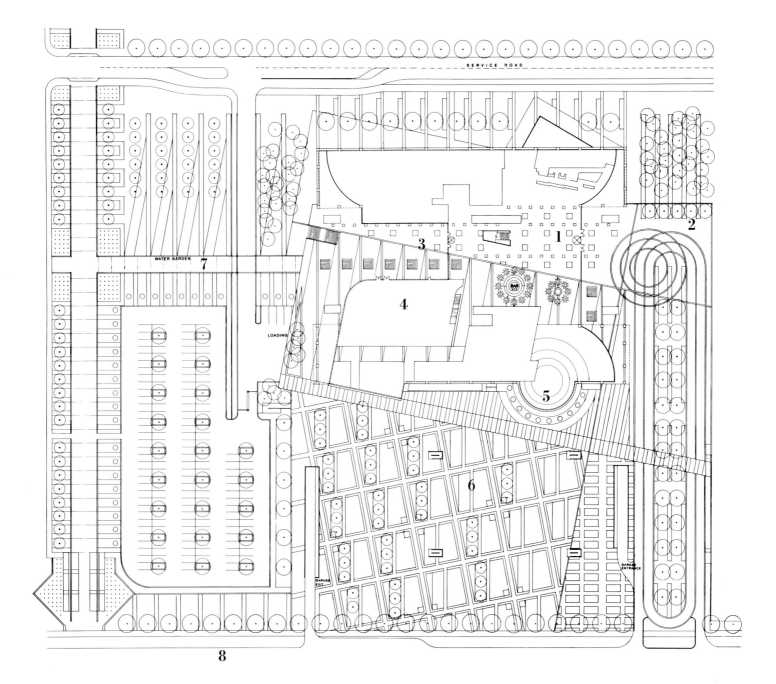

The concept for the major parterre garden of Murphy/Jahn's Kempinski Hotel building in Munich is based on the created order of one orthogonal grid defied by another, overlapping grid. Because these angles have no reference in the landscape, they refocus the inter-relationship of their own forms in the space and, in turn, make the observer's point of view an internal reference in scale and orientation. These complex layers are articulated by patterns of low boxwood hedges, colored gravels, columnar oaks, and lawn. The turning angles can be viewed not only from the atrium and terrace of the hotel, but also from the rooms and offices above, as well as from within. Curtain walls of glass move diagonally through the interior spaces. Abstracted geometric "trees," placed like elements in a modern stage set, act to enliven and forest the shimmering space.

Angled parterre

Parterre with hedges, grass, gravel, and oak

Parterre garden over garage

Atrium garden gestures through glass curtain

Atrium garden with geranium cases

Monumental glass cases with potted geraniums

Beer garden "trees"

"Palm" grove

Sony Makuhari Technology Center and Toyosuna Park

Location: Makuhari, Chiba Prefecture, Japan
Client: Sony Corporation
Architect: Kunihide Oshinomi, Kajima Design
Landscape
Architect: Peter Walker William Johnson and Partners
Proposal: 1991

For a Sony Corporation office building and research center designed by Kunihide Oshinomi of Kajima Design with a geometric exoskeleton based on a system of grids, Peter Walker William Johnson and Partners chose to combine the traditionally rich Japanese materials of gravel, sand, stone, hedges, and water with the modern technological elements of video monitors to make an overlapping gridded ground plane.

Reiterating the repeated squares of the intricate building, the landscape design uses terraces patterned with small squares of water and sand creating a stylized beach. Video monitors are placed systematically in the garden both to acknowledge the contemporary, technological identity of the client and to

1 Research buildings
2 Restaurant
3 Sony store
4 Video garden
5 Reflection pool
6 Toyosuna Park

0 ——————— 30 meters

View across Toyosuna Park

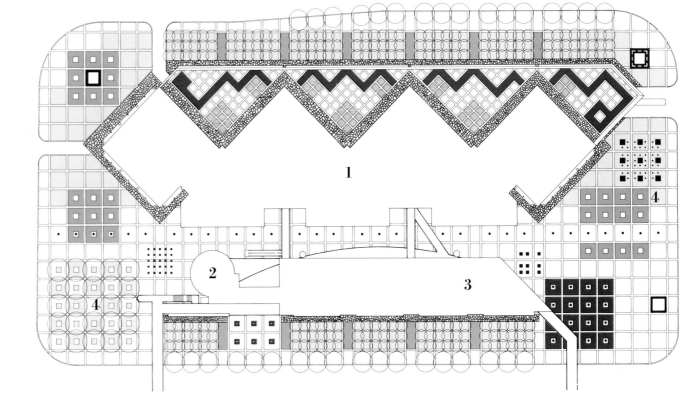

incorporate the pattern of the overall design. Walkways and the arcade extend from the building and garden to the adjacent Toyosuna Park.

The schematic landscape design for Toyosuna Park is a continuation of the pedestrian axis of Sony's public garden. Promenades, seating areas, children's play spaces, and a majestic reflecting pool are woven into the matrix of two large groves of deciduous and flowering trees. This "technological forest," employing modern reforestation techniques, combines the mathematical precision of the computer age and traditional park materials for a unique and memorable landscape.

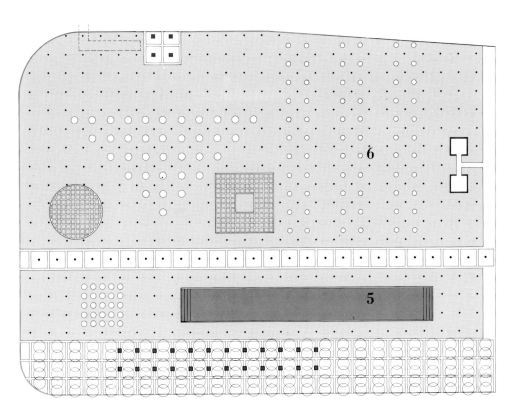

Plaza garden with video "flowers"

Vertical allée through park

Marugame Station Plaza

Location: Marugame Genichiro-Inokuma
Museum of Contemporary Art (MIMOCA),
Marugame City, Kagawa Prefecture, Japan
Client: Marugame City
Urban
Designer: Gen Kato, Nihon-Toshi-Sogo-Kenkyusho
Architect: Taniguchi and Associates (MIMOCA)
Landscape
Architect: Peter Walker and Partners
Toshi-Keikan-Sekkie, Inc.,
Landscape construction observation
Completed: 1992

1 Train station
2 Art museum with library below
3 Fountain
4 Boulders
5 Future shopping center

0   40 meters

Marugame Station Plaza presented the unusual opportunity of designing an urban public plaza in Japan to serve the Marugame train station, planned by Gen Kato, and the new MIMOCA museum and library, designed by Yoshio Taniguchi. One of the concepts of Peter Walker and Partners was to provide a plan that would effectively link the prevailing disparate spaces and activities. To this task, Walker added the idea of involving the architecture and the existing varied environment in the work resolution, by imposing the logic of a repetitive system (in this case, an organized paving pattern) on the street, connecting pavements and walkways.

With invented patterning, composed of sections of the fine cobbled stones used in ancient Japanese gardens alternating at regular and repeated intervals with the common asphalt of the surrounding modern roadway, the previously "empty" spaces in and between the existing architecture were transformed into an unmistakably unified and visible zone. Context for this striped marking of a space to identify it as a solid and yet fluid totality can also be found in Burle Marx's work in Rio at the Copacabana and in the architecturally related installation work of the French conceptualist Daniel Buren. This system of patterned markings effectively usurps the power and memory of the previous, familiar environment, enabling a new perception of the site.

Once this overall system was in place, Peter Walker and Partners installed a series of carefully conceived and fabricated individual elements that attest to their commitment to the nobility of the functional. As a symbol of entry into the city, a fountain was created and sited in a round pool. Composed of four identical painted steel rectangles, the fountain contains flat sheets of water that "rain" inside each frame and then flow into the pool. This image, inspired by traditional Torii Gates of entry in Japan and by the crane structures used in the high-tech shipping industry that is part of the city's port activity, becomes an element of the internal system that echoes the tempo of the entire plan.

A snaking line of identical fabricated fiberglass rocks provides another dynamic image for the plaza. These rocks, used for seating and as bollards to protect pedestrians from vehicular traffic, glow from within with a warm orange-red light at dawn and at nightfall. The lights, along with others that outline the shapes and forms of the design in the dark, add color and movement to the plan. One end of the line of rocks is purposefully curved into a spiral form, providing a rhythmic counterpoint to the regular spacing of the pavement throughout the plaza.

Stone spiral

Asphalt, cobbles, and slate paving

Rain lines in pool

Fountain at dusk

"Stone" seat bollards

"Stones" glow at night with museum porch beyond

Rain layers fountain

"Torii" gateway and "container crane" fountain

Europa-Haus

Location: Frankfurt, Germany
Client: SkanInvest
Architect: Murphy/Jahn, Inc., Architects
Landscape
Architect: Peter Walker William Johnson and Partners
Proposal: 1992

1 Office
2 Residential
3 Frankfurter benches
4 Cafe
5 Fountain
6 Escalators
7 Service road

0   200 meters

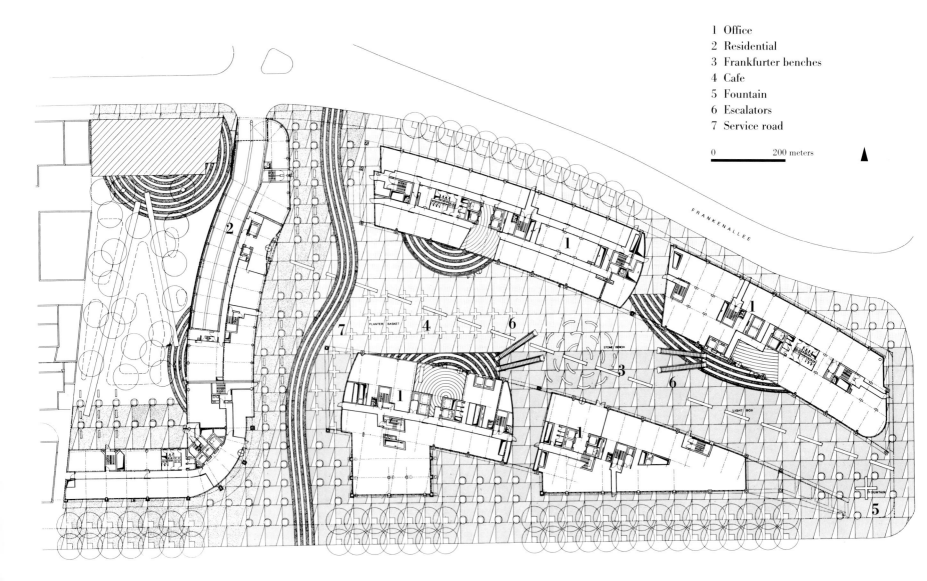

Europa-Haus is a fine example of Peter Walker William Johnson and Partners' use of a serial structure, here defined as an overall framework that contains similar and repeated units installed in a consistent relationship. Although repeated rhythms in music, dance, architecture, and the landscape are found throughout history, modern use of serial imagery in the visual arts is traced from Claude Monet's late-nineteenth-century series of *Haystacks*, *Poplars*, and the Cathedral paintings. In these works, Monet examined and reexamined the subtleties of the shifts in nature, especially those precipitated by shifts of light and season, and of our perceptions of these changes. Modern art history contains a prominent strain of exploration of the serial as a clue to the understanding of nature and the universe. Walker's work extends this inquiry with an inclusive language encompassing the arts, philosophy, spirituality, the practical and designed in the arena of public gardens and landscapes.

The methodology of the Europa-Haus garden is to contrast the interior space and a richly patterned urban floor with the central, Gothic planes created by the sculptural Helmut Jahn buildings. Responding to the template of the architectural details, this space, overlaid with small paving blocks traditional to German streets, is meant to be seen from within and above as a great urban room, appointed with objects and plants as a giant interior lobby space might be. The patterning reveals a subtle and progressive change of color to distinguish the various districts in the garden. Like staff paper to lively musical notation, the patterned floor functions as a consistent rhythmic foil for the vibrantly diverse activities central to the plan.

Reflecting Walker's idea of positioning objects in space and space within objects, the overall plan for Europa-Haus incorporates a number of highlighted and individual gestures. A sculptural line of light marks the floor of the central space and dramatically bisects it, creating a visual focus and eliciting a subtle, perceptual awareness of its direction. Dramatically designed and placed escalators to the second floor entrances of the buildings serve as dimensional radiants on the essential ground motif. As with the majority of components of the plan, these accord function as well as being significant to the design. A series of cruciform planters of ivy, forming their own primary shape and sequence, is used to define the space of an outdoor cafe. Serving as benches, seats, and mazes for children's play, rounded carved stones in the form of giant frankfurters are placed in concentric circles, distinguishing another area of the multifaceted garden. The overt and humorous play of "frankfurters" in Frankfurt as a visual and literal pun punctuates the space.

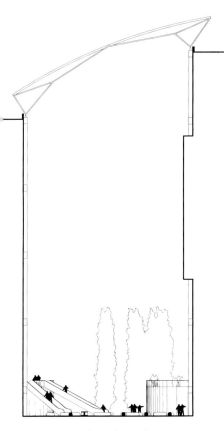

Cross section through arcade

Mosaic plaza floor with cafe and stainless steel line of lights

Curved terrazzo service road

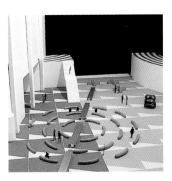

Stone frankfurter benches

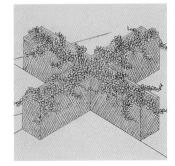

Ivy planters

Euralille Parc Urbain

Location: *Lille, France*
Client: *City of Lille*
Architect: *Rem Koolhaas, Master Planner*
Competition
Team: *Peter Walker William Johnson and Partners*
         Pascale Jacotot, Paysagiste
         DPLG, Paris
Drawings: *William Johnson*
Competition: *1992*

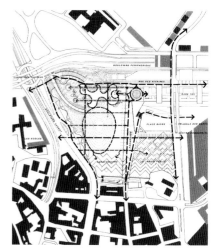

The Parc related to the historic city

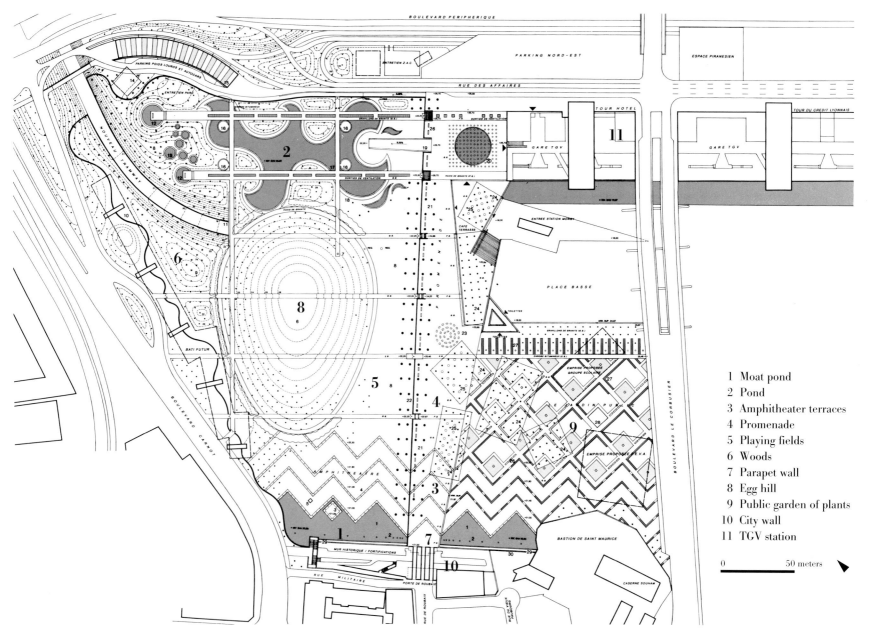

1   Moat pond
2   Pond
3   Amphitheater terraces
4   Promenade
5   Playing fields
6   Woods
7   Parapet wall
8   Egg hill
9   Public garden of plants
10   City wall
11   TGV station

0   50 meters

In a project identified with the movement of history and culture into the next century, Peter Walker William Johnson and Partners teamed with French urban designers to offer a vision of the transformation of the provincial town of Lille, located in northeastern France near its shared border with Belgium, into a megalopolitan vision of the twenty-first century. Sponsored by public and private funds and with the renowned Dutch architect Rem Koolhaas serving as master planner, the new massive Business Center is to include a number of grand-scaled structures by internationally recognized architects; a station for the advanced, high-speed TGV trains that will connect Lille with London and Paris; and substantial spaces devoted to retail, residential, hotel, office, cultural, and park facilities.

As a crucial aspect of this hub for business and technologically sophisticated international infrastructure, Peter Walker William Johnson and Partners proposed a park featuring a promenade linking the TGV station area with the old city of Lille, a hill highlighted by a wooded park, and a public garden. These elements of the park design would effectively serve the millions of people likely to frequent Euralille, while providing a real sense of community through a human-scale concept for Euralille Parc.

Intending to create a spirit that is forward-looking while acknowledging Lille's rich, medieval past, the public garden is laid out with gridded paths, hedges, chestnut and cherry trees, and individual garden rooms in collaged patterns evocative of Lille's historic textile production. A central, rolling hill, formed in an elliptical egg shape that offers a sense of mystery and whimsy, features a grove of willows, creating both privacy within the park and an inclusive transparency. A large amphitheater and its chevron-patterned terraces extend into the park, providing energy and movement directed both toward the park and across the rebuilt moat to the old city. A grand promenade lined with trees and benches and a sound and light kiosk are additional aspects meant to enliven the community and cultural essence of the space. Despite the grand scale of the plan, Walker is careful to consistently envision spaces for individuals and small groups or families to experience the familiar intimacy of a park.

Moat at edge of historic city wall

Grand promenade to station

Hill and playing fields

Public garden of plants

153

Longacres Park–
The Boeing Company

Location: Renton, Washington
Client: The Boeing Company
Architect: Skidmore, Owings & Merrill, San Francisco
Engineer: Sverdrup
Wetland
Consultant: L.C. Lee & Associates
Landscape
Architect: Peter Walker William Johnson and Partners
Bruce Dees & Associates,
Landscape construction documents

Phase One
completed: 1994

1 Parking
2 Training center
3 Administration
4 Offices
5 Dining commons
6 Wetland lake
7 Forest

0   800 feet   ▼

A collaborative team led by Skidmore, Owings & Merrill and Peter Walker William Johnson and Partners approached the task of redeveloping a 212-acre site in the Pacific Northwest of the United States with ambitious goals. These include conversion of a former racetrack to an environmentally sensitive urbanized area, an office campus of seventeen buildings organized around a central open space, restoration of a major wetland, and a contemporary design scheme that references the region's previous agricultural use.

A fluid schematic design of the park results from the dynamic features of re-creating a wetland system with a 6-acre lake, a 4-acre marsh, and new streams and ponds. This sculpting with land and water proved an experimental innovation for Peter Walker William Johnson and Partners, leading to new directions still being explored. An aesthetic counterpoint to the organic shapes and contours of the wetlands is the overlay of a geometric, stylized "forest" of native evergreen and deciduous trees throughout the site. The element of a diagonal grid visually relates to the imposing Mount Rainier in the distance.

Proposed new forest and wetlands

Complex wetland stream

Terrace at training center

Path with log edging

Bridge over pond

Water lilies align with Mt. Ranier

University of California at San Diego Library Walk

Location: *San Diego, California*
Client: *University of California at San Diego*
Landscape
Architect: *Peter Walker William Johnson and Partners*
Completed: *1995*

Existing eucalyptus groves

1 Library Walk
2 Student Center
3 Classroom building
4 Medical School
5 Library
6 Eucalyptus grove
7 Future classroom building

0   100 feet

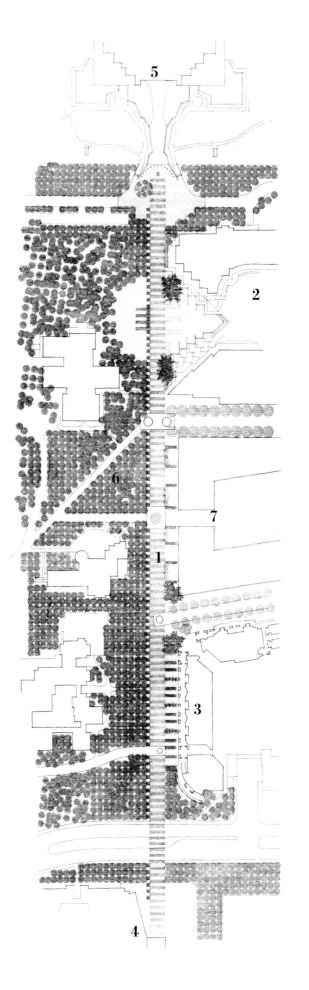

*View of Walk toward
Medical School*

Night view

Walk at new classroom building

Seating area beside Walk

*Unit paved stripes with new
eucalyptus planting*

Precast concrete bench lanterns

Built on bluffs above the Pacific Ocean in Southern California, this University of California campus possesses mature groves of majestic eucalyptus forming the forest that surrounds many of the campus buildings. On this campus, the University has carefully assembled an internationally respected collection of outdoor sculpture and land art, many sited among the trees.

With the task of creating a major linear space that will join the newly enlarged library with a series of other campus buildings, Peter Walker William Johnson and Partners also addresses the need for a spatial structure that will unify some of the diverse aspects of the previous campus design. Integrating this space with existing paths and walks, the plan offers the development of the major axis as a strong and independent statement in itself.

Using a distinctive composition of alternating patterns in the pavement, in the bold, directive manner that French artist Daniel Buren might, the new central paved walkway works as a unifying force and a plazalike focus for the campus. Walls for sitting, platforms for public speaking, and adjacent spaces for meeting are included. Part of the design also calculates to augment vistas into the nearby forest, as well as to preserve and reinforce the grid by planting new trees.

As with many of the office's projects, lighting is key to this scheme. The speaking platforms become beacons and lanterns in the evening, when lighting from below illuminates the platforms, the path, and the forest. These points of light help to mark the axial line of the pavement, reinforcing the strength of the synthesizing central place of passage.

Toyota Municipal Museum of Art

Location: Toyota City, Aichi Prefecture, Japan
Client: Toyota City Government
Architect: Taniguchi and Associates
Landscape
Architect: Peter Walker William Johnson and Partners
              Kazumi Mizoguchi Landscape Office
Completed: 1995

New stone stair to historic
tea house

Entry with Richard Serra sculpture

 1 Pond
 2 Fountain
 3 Main walk
 4 Arrival court
 5 Tea house
 6 Castle
 7 Sculpture gardens
 8 Museum
 9 Slate path
10 Forest
11 Parking
12 Viewing terrace

0   20 meters

The gardens and grounds of the new Toyota Municipal Museum of Art provide a microcosm of the issues of presenting the development of art in a historical perspective: how to site the modern work in a context that includes earlier and even ancient art. With the new and old structures of the project as a metaphor for a museum that holds art from diverse historical periods in its collection, the landscape design of the Toyota Municipal Museum of Art serves as the unifying element for the complex, which includes the refined modernist composition of the new museum building by Taniguchi and Associates, the adjacent traditional tea house and garden, and a historic castle and forest.

Peter Walker William Johnson and Partners confronted this quandary with a plan for the outdoor spaces as a combination of distinct yet interrelated areas, providing connection and dialogue within a unified whole. While addressing the modernist building with a contemporary vision, the plan also offers respect and protection for the earlier components, with both literal and historical access among all parts.

For the museum area, the ground plane, consisting of garden parterres, paved plazas, a water garden, a pond, and forest edge, is ordered by transformations of a single geometry. Gesturing back and forth from the museum to the castle are two stone paths: one linking the museum and castle entrances, the other an indirect connection edging the lake. As counterpoint, an eccentrically placed slate pathway and an irregular stone wall at the lake edge ramble independently in the formally organized ground plane, tempering the regularity of the composition to allow for a more open and inclusive entity.

The project also necessitates a meticulous restoration of the tea garden and the gardens surrounding the castle. Connections and integrating elements are accentuated in the plan, and the subtleties of the dialogue between old and new are considered throughout: the entrance walkway to the new museum, while proportionally designed to the modernist scale of the new structure, uses irregular paving stones that relate to those of the ancient castle. These integrating elements are conceived carefully so as to harmonize the need for spatial autonomy that the different structures and gardens require.

Pond at viewing terrace

Main stone walk

Sculpture garden court with Richard Serra sculpture

Garden with Henry Moore and Arnaldo Pomodoro sculptures

Air fountain

Air fountain at dusk

Path, stone wall, and pool

Sculpture garden with forest beyond

Principal Mutual Life Insurance Company, Corporate Expansion

Location: *Des Moines, Iowa*
Client: *Principal Financial Group*
Architect: *Murphy/Jahn, Inc., Architects*
Landscape
Architect: *Peter Walker William Johnson*
         and Partners
Completed: *1996*

1 Fountain/stage
2 Promenade
3 Cafe
4 Great lawn
5 Light wall
6 Sitting garden
7 Rock garden

0   64 feet

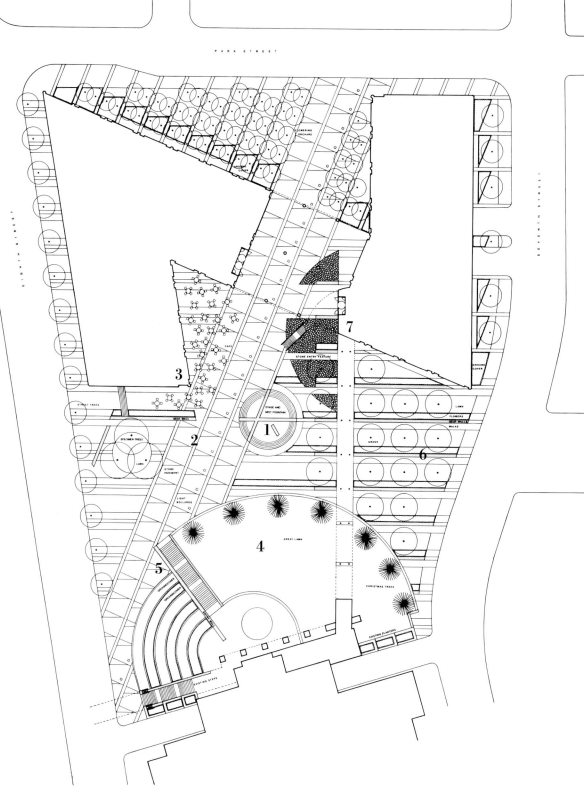

The plaza for the new Murphy/Jahn structure for Principal Mutual Life Insurance Company's corporate expansion was approached by Peter Walker William Johnson and Partners as an assemblage of different textures, colors, materials, and spatial forms. The collaged composition consists of a geometrically patterned palette of stone for the plaza and a garden designed with grids of flower beds, lawn, oak trees, and stone benches. These geometric frameworks are oriented to the opposing grids of the city's own design. At the center of the plan, existing half in the plaza and half in the garden, is a circular glass stage that consolidates the energy of the entire scheme in its simple and direct form. When not used as a stage, this median surface becomes a fountain of mist creating hovering clouds that refract lights from below.

Sitting garden from above

Stage and mist fountain

Great lawn with lantern wall

Plaza passage through building

Complex paving at plaza

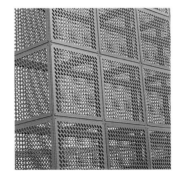
Detail of lantern wall

Lantern wall

Stage with mist fountain

Harima Science Garden City

Location: Hyogo Prefecture, Japan
Client: Hyogo Prefectural Government, Public Enterprise Agency
Urban Design
Team: A.D.H. Architects, Urban Design Team Coordinator
Architect: Arata Isozaki and Associates
Landscape
Architect: Peter Walker William Johnson and Partners HEADS Co., Ltd.
Lighting: Lighting Planners Associates, Inc.
Street Furnishings
and Signage: G. K. Sekkei Associates
Drawings: William Johnson
Completed: 1993

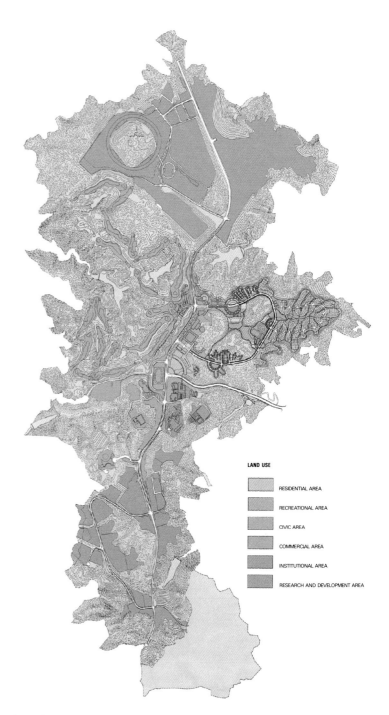

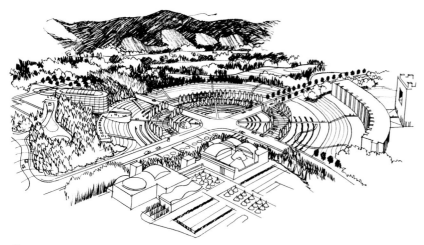

Town center

LAND USE

RESIDENTIAL AREA

RECREATIONAL AREA

CIVIC AREA

COMMERCIAL AREA

INSTITUTIONAL AREA

RESEARCH AND DEVELOPMENT AREA

Land use plan

Working with architect Arata Isozaki and Associates and others to form an urban design team, Peter Walker William Johnson and Partners had the mandate of creating a master plan for the 5,000-acre Harima Science Garden City, a new town now under construction in a mountainous interior valley of Japan. Repairing the natural landscape that had been stripped of much of its forests was at the essence of the concept for this new scientific community.

While designing the city with the environmental and technical concerns the project required, Arata Isozaki and Peter Walker also considered the joint endeavor an opportunity for artistic dialogue. The vision they shared was that of an original response to the land and to culture, both historical and contemporary. The forward-looking scientific work to be done in the new city, along with the focus on its recreational offerings, suggested a confluence of ideas and technology.

Town Park, the literal and symbolic axis of the town, marks the intersection of the major streets and the distinct residential, commercial, institutional, and recreational components of Harima Science Garden City with the single and simple form of the circle. Emblematic of the center of the town, the circle is a pure form meant to be examined spatially for its richness. From within and without, above and below, in and around, and turning, the geometry of the circle is explored to the extent that it heightens our awareness of the power of its form. As the point of view is changed, so is the spatial reference to which we are oriented.

The visual and actual events that occur in and around the circle of Town Park are entirely focused on recreational and outdoor activities. Along with emphasizing the significance of the form, this area of recreation provides the town with a center for its spirit.

As primitive imagery employed the circle on the land to conjure magical powers, so artists have used the circle throughout history to connect their expressions to primary forms and forces in the universe. Endowing a segment of the earth with the shape of the sun and moon reflects and invokes that nexus.

Stone wall and pond at base of buildings

Snake stream through bamboo "forest"

Stepped ponds at stone wall

Lower stream pond

Stainless steel willow island in pond

Waterfall at stone wall step

Snake head at face of bamboo "forest"

Snake stream

Center for the Advanced Science and Technology

Location: Hyogo Prefecture, Japan
Client: Hyogo Prefectural Government,
                 Public Enterprise Agency
Urban Design
Team: A.D.H. Architects,
                 Urban Design Team Coordinator
Architect: Arata Isozaki and Associates
Landscape
Architect: Peter Walker William Johnson and Partners
                 HEADS Co., Ltd.
Lighting: Lighting Planners Associates, Inc.
Street Furnishings
and Signage: G. K. Sekkei Associates
Completed: 1993

1   Volcano garden
2   Ryokan garden
3   Snake stream
4   Bridge to housing
5   Stepped ponds
6   Promenade
7   University
8   Housing
9   Conference center
10 Guest house

View over wall of Ryokan garden

Parking lot and "Volcano" garden

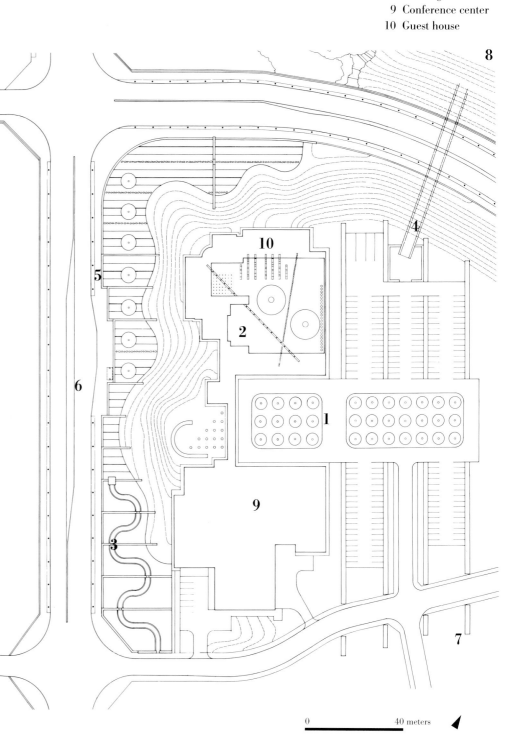

0   40 meters

Responding to the landmark Arata Isozaki building that houses the Center for the Advanced Science and Technology (CAST), the gardens of the CAST building demonstrate a distinctive ordering and a reflective wit rarely seen in public art. Walker invented a systemic village of grassy mounds that appear more like a theatrical set than any familiar garden. Contrasted with the forested mountains that surround Harima, this "Volcano" garden presents a formal and monumental succession of stylized foothills, each adorned with a cypress tree ignited with a little red bulb at the top.

The extraordinary aspect of this garden is its chameleonlike transformations: at times it seems a regimented whimsy, reading like the playground of a giant. Monumental qualities convey it as a signal with some mysterious coding for viewers from the sky. When darkness falls, the lot becomes a strange night forest, with the red lights an eerie and yet welcome beam of recognition. When the fog moves in, there is magical poetry to the erect cypresses, as if a series of lines drawn in the air. The many interpretations of this one simple installation offer an understanding of the human urge to make a line, the link between the early primitive cave markings and these sophisticated drawings in space.

Another garden is located in the interior courtyard of the Isozaki building. Primarily meant for contemplation, this garden nevertheless draws us in so we figuratively move through the alluring space as we observe and examine its components.

The garden is composed of a sea of raked gravel from which rise two huge mountains, one of stone and one of moss, which infuse the space with surrealistic scale. A little forest of bamboo holds a section of the garden with mist rising through it. Stone and ancient wooden stepping-stones dissect and traverse the garden floor. With a quiet power reflective of traditional Japanese meditation gardens, this modern expression also portrays a theatrical magic in its scale and its refined composition.

The gardens of the Center for the Advanced Science and Technology represent an excellent example of Walker's mature work. His affinity with minimal art, his urge to record human observation, his reaching for the more primitive and universal connections between earth and sky are eminently demonstrated in these works. Such powerful qualities are achieved without loosing a certain detached humor that pervades the best of Walker's gardens.

"Volcano" garden

Ryokan "mountain" garden

Mist fountain in Ryokan garden

Stone and moss "mountains"

Stones and burnt logs

Polished stone "piers"

Lines of ancient burnt logs and stones

Stones and raked sand

McConnell Foundation

Location: *Redding, California*
Client: *McConnell Foundation*
Architect: *NBBJ Architects*
Landscape
Architect: *Peter Walker William Johnson and Partners*
Projected
completion: *1997*

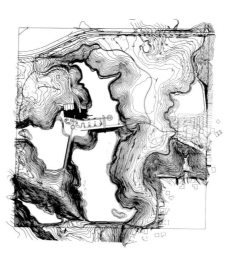

0   500 feet ◀

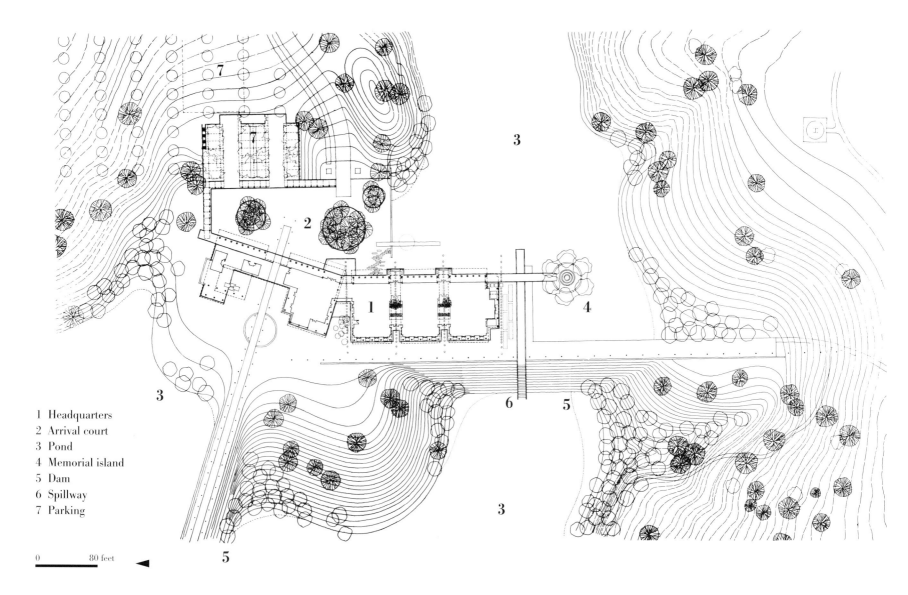

1 Headquarters
2 Arrival court
3 Pond
4 Memorial island
5 Dam
6 Spillway
7 Parking

0   80 feet ◀

Sited on 150 acres in Redding, California, at the northern end of the Sacramento Valley near the foot of the spectacular Sierra Nevada, the new headquarters for the philanthropic McConnell Foundation offered a major challenge and opportunity for Peter Walker William Johnson and Partners. Stripped of the beauty of its native ecology by previous earth moving and extensive overgrazing, the landscape task included major repair of the site to achieve the land's own inherent potential.

With native grassland and wetland ecosystems in need of significant restoration, on-site ponds requiring draining and reshaping, and a memorial and more intimate gardens to be realized as an interior focus for the expansive design, Peter Walker William Johnson and Partners worked closely with Seattle based NBBJ Architects to return integrity and vitality to the property. These changes, requiring a substantial movement of land and water more typically associated with civil engineering than with landscape projects, and extensive reestablishment of native plants and trees, represent the synergy of ecology and art, a complex congruence of geometry and the re-creation of natural beauty that was all but lost. The grand scope of the project allows for and necessitates an array of ecological, artistic, and functional responses.

McConnell Foundation is approached by an entrance road that snakes informally through a persimmon orchard with a view of blue oak and madrone trees offering an exotic and spectacular landscape. The drive terminates at a path where linear, water-washed stone slabs are set in sand leading to a stone plaza. At the entrance, one has an immediate encounter with an ephemeral mist fountain sited at the end of a stone pier extending into the nearby pond. Upon entering the complex, the visitor finds another fountain, this one animated with bubbles generated from air-pumping jets below. The activation of water is a theme carried over from the three natural ponds, integrating the man-made with the natural.

The one-story, linear building constitutes a rural yet formal structure sited at the juncture of the ponds, interacting at every turn and view with the water, the meadows, the landscape, and mountains beyond. Paths of stepping-stones (gleaned from local streambeds) run east to west from the pond through the interior of the structure and onto the lawn, providing the conceptual and literal cohesion between water and land that is a key element of the design.

Two dams abutting the building furnish a primary geometry, articulating a central angle that grounds the predominantly curvilinear extensions of the landscape. Compounding the central angularity, a fountain spillway connects two of the ponds with a smaller right angled channel, which, in turn, intersects a yet smaller linear path to the spherical memorial island. The essentially subtle geometry incorporates an allée of olive trees, a column-lined arcade, and three circular fountains within the nucleus of the design. These circles and angles reappear throughout the gardens in proximity to the building, formulating a plan within the plan, and, like a play within a play, adding metaphor and symbol.

The special memorial island honoring the McConnell Foundation founders is approached by a flagstone walkway. Consisting of a flat lawn encircled for privacy by a ring of larch trees and a circular stone seat wall, the island garden divulges a central fountain with concentric alternating rings of polished black granite and still water. This is a peaceful, meditative place formed for intimacy and quiet.

The explicit design elements sustain form within the greater environment of organic growth, identifying the McConnell Foundation as nature interfaced with the mind and hand of artists.

*Rebuilt main dam with
headquarters building*

Main dam with spillway

Existing site with three ponds

Founders memorial island

Headquarters on upper pond

Power Plants

Location: International Garden Festival
                Château Chaumont-sur-Loire, France
Landscape
Architect: Peter Walker William Johnson and Partners
                Charles Dard Paysagiste, Paris
Sponsor: Conservatoire des Parcs et Jardins et du Paysage
Temporarily
installed: 1993

1 Solar panel
2 Deck chair
3 Sunflowers
4 Fluorescent light

For the 1993 International Garden Festival in Chaumont-sur-Loire, France, Peter Walker created a garden that offered a witty pun on first view. Striped lawn chairs, each with a solar panel behind it, were placed on gravel pads spaced regularly within a field of sunflowers. The implication and associations of sunbathing, solar/sun energy collecting and dispersing, and sunflowers growing were layered within the visual and metaphoric pun. The garden offered a more serious intent, however, in its effort to manifest a display of nature and technology in service to each other. The solar panels also functioned as a power source for the central fluorescent line that served as a design component, drawing the eye to the heart of the sunflower garden while also lighting the garden.

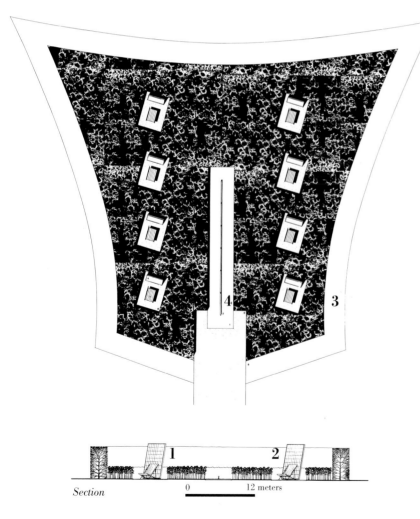

Section   0   12 meters

Fluorescent light powered by
solar panels

Solar panels and deck chairs

Solar panels

Sunflowers and solar panels

Ground Covers

Location: Escondido, California;
temporary installation for
"California: In Three Dimensions" at the
California Center for the Arts Museum

Landscape
Architect: Peter Walker William Johnson and Partners
Temporarily
installed: 1995

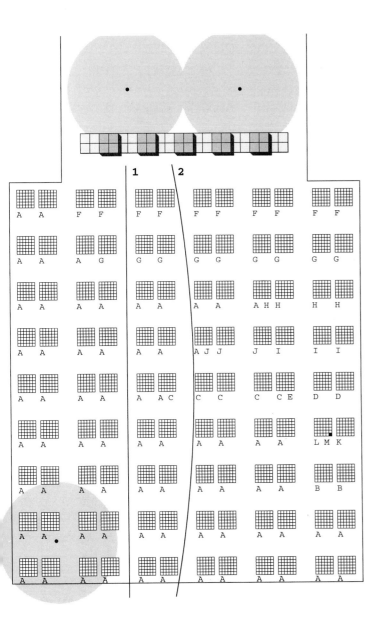

In considering the designed landscapes of Peter Walker, traditional ideas about garden making are better put aside for a broader understanding of landscape as a vehicle for art making. Walker's artistic vocabulary for creating a visible landscape focuses on a formal and classical ordering while also communicating the universality of our desire to acknowledge and relate to the greater environment.

Walker's work *Ground Covers*, a site-specific installation for "California: In Three Dimensions," an exhibition at the California Center for the Arts Museum, Escondido, California, in the summer of 1995, is composed of a visual system of regular planes. These are formed by nursery flats containing materials that reiterate the actual percentages of the earth's surface covered by fresh and salt water, ice, forests, deserts, grasslands, gardens and farmlands, and urban areas. The overall placement of these cultivated units reveals its own inherent rhythm and pattern, along with some surprising conclusions about what actually constitutes our surroundings. Two lines of concrete blocks dissect the plan, one representing the actual curvature of the earth, the other exhibiting the same curvature in profile, exaggerated multifold.

Implying clues to its visual, ecological, phenomenological, and philosophical underpinnings, *Ground Covers* offers an overlay of commentary on the state of the earth and our relationship to the environment. Along with the specific intent of portraying these observations, the work also offers aspects of a composed and traditional garden where the viewer can stroll, contemplating both the reality and the ideal of nature as it exists and as we have created it by our own alterations.

A	Salt Water	67.0%
B	Salt Water—Oil Slicks	1.2%
C	Fresh Water—Frozen	3.2%
D	Fresh Water	2.0%
E	Fresh Water—Polluted	0.3%
F	Desert	9.0%
G	Forest	8.3%
H	Grass Land	3.0%
I	Agriculture	3.0%
J	Agriculture—Degraded Land	2.0%
K	Urban	0.52%
L	Urban—Industrial Degraded Land	0.46%
M	Gardens and Parks	0.02%

Line "1" represents the actual curvature of the earth.
Line "2" represents the curvature of the earth in profile exaggerated 190,224 times.
The scale of the surface of the earth to *Ground Covers* is 15,125,760,000:1.
One 3-inch planting cell is equal to approximately 50,740 square miles.

0   11 feet

Installation view toward the
museum

Installation view with benches

Singapore Performing Arts Center

Location: *Singapore*
Client: *Government of Singapore*
Architect: *Michael Wilford and Partners, Ltd., London*
D.P. Architects PTE, Ltd., Singapore
Landscape
Architect: *Peter Walker William Johnson and Partners*
Clouston, Singapore
Proposal: *1994*

For Singapore's world-class Performing Arts Center scheduled to open at the cusp of the new century, Peter Walker William Johnson and Partners teamed with Michael Wilford and Partners, Ltd., London, and D.P. Architects PTE, Ltd., Singapore, to unfold a definitive and emblematic design of that rich and diverse cultural community.

The center is sited in a substantial perimeter of preserved green along the city and waterfronts of Singapore, connecting key areas of the historic and contemporary city. The center's clear mandate is to provide a place of convergence for the traditional and innovative arts of the Asian cultures that intersect in Singapore.

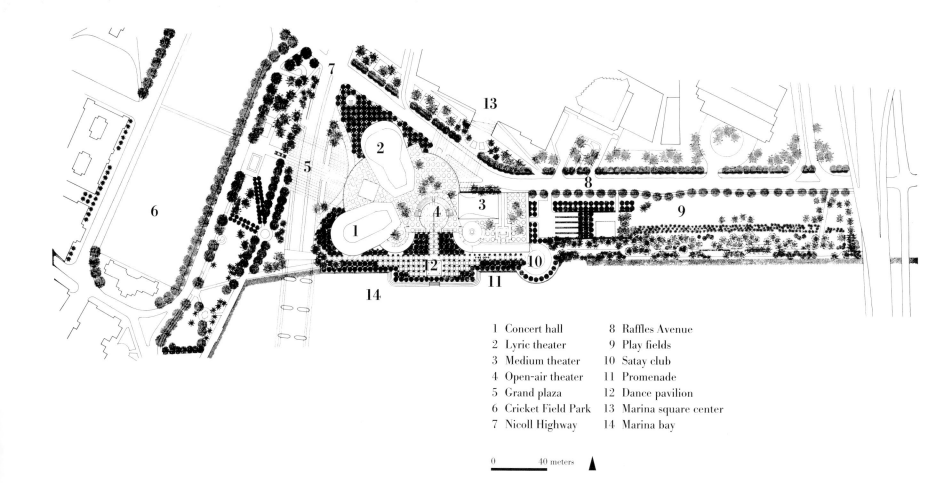

1	Concert hall	8	Raffles Avenue
2	Lyric theater	9	Play fields
3	Medium theater	10	Satay club
4	Open-air theater	11	Promenade
5	Grand plaza	12	Dance pavilion
6	Cricket Field Park	13	Marina square center
7	Nicoll Highway	14	Marina bay

0   40 meters

The complexity of the design of the landscape and gardens echoes the composite mix of the political and cultural intertwining that is part of the history of Singapore. It also serves to extend the function and beauty of the architecture, by actuating an integrated flow of energy and space in the center's indoor and outdoor realms.

The plan for Singapore represents the next step in Peter Walker's evolving idea of using a formal design as a vehicle not only for ordering and transposing, but for ultimately generating a more mysterious, intuitive environment. In the three-dimensional matrix of this urban garden, a tall gridded top canopy of palms or Norfolk Island pines is above a middle, flowering underlayer of shade-producing cassia trees. The lowest, ground level pattern of large, finely cut, circular granite stones, alternating with fine grasses and an internal system of smaller cobbles, forms a textural carpet. Each element of the matrix contains its own variations and complexities, as it interrelates with the various grids and the architecture in a kind of visual and physical dance activated in the overall rhythm of the landscape design. The vertical scale of the palms is reflected in the glass-skinned performance halls on the harbor side, optically extending the existing green park along the esplanades and reaching out toward the colonial-era Cricket Field Park. In addition to being set flush with the ground, the 15-foot-diameter stones are raised to provide seating, and the forms are repeated again in a series of stone-walled reflecting pools.

The grasses and cobbles themselves serve multipurposes, creating a delicate pattern of their own and offering a canvas for unpredictability. People walking in the gardens will wear impromptu paths through the grasses, offering a random counterpoint to the more regulated components of the design.

Continuing the experiencing of the Center, a forest of stainless steel wands is envisioned at the height of the automobile entrance, each wand revealing a small incandescent light exactly matching the light patterns on the underside of the building canopy. This plane of sparkling lights provides a welcoming, magical flicker at night, and extends the lights of the canopy across each boulevard and then back into the lobby spaces of each structure.

A final unity in the plan is the extension of the stone-and-grass carpet onto the roof terraces between the great halls, becoming lively green pedestrian promenades with additional space for performances and magnificent views of the harbor and the city.

Palm and low cassia grid

Norfolk Island pine and low cassia grid

Raised stone disks beneath double-layered tree canopy

Geometric density of double orchard

Shaded stone seating area

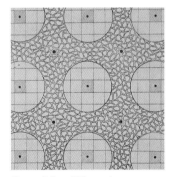

Stone disk, cobble, and grass paving

Stralauer Platz Park

Location: *Berlin, Germany*
Client: *OPUS Corporation*
Architect: *Murphy/Jahn, Inc., Architects*
Landscape
Architect: *Peter Walker William Johnson and Partners*
Projected
completion: *1998*

Park promenade along the River Spree

Segment of Berlin Wall

As their proposal in a postreunification competition in Berlin, Germany, Murphy/Jahn, Inc., Architects and Peter Walker William Johnson and Partners presented a major plan for a building on Stralauer Platz and a commemorative park on adjacent, previously derelict land.

Helmut Jahn's design for this structure effectively indicates the many directions that congealed to move Berlin into the twenty-first century, as it offers an important architectural statement in a city dedicated to rebuilding its vision.

The Murphy/Jahn edifice is a glass-sheathed, transparent pavilion facing both bordering streets and the River

Spree, which flows through the city. Designed as a great, spinning pinwheel to integrate its multidimensional surroundings, it opens into a cross-axial plaza that links the street to the river, and offers passage for riders of the nearby train station as well.

The landscape design of the project is composed of two connected yet distinct gardens, one relating directly to the Murphy/Jahn structure and the other a major public green park. As an initial motif orchestrating the cohesion of the open spaces, a series of four reflecting pools, starting in the building plaza and extending through the actual structure and its grand atrium, progresses to the green riverfront park beyond. Each pool

1 River Spree
2 Fountains
3 Promenade
4 Plaza
5 Winter Garden
6 Playground
7 Berlin Wall
8 Trolley bridge
9 Amphitheater
10 Train station
11 Boat landing

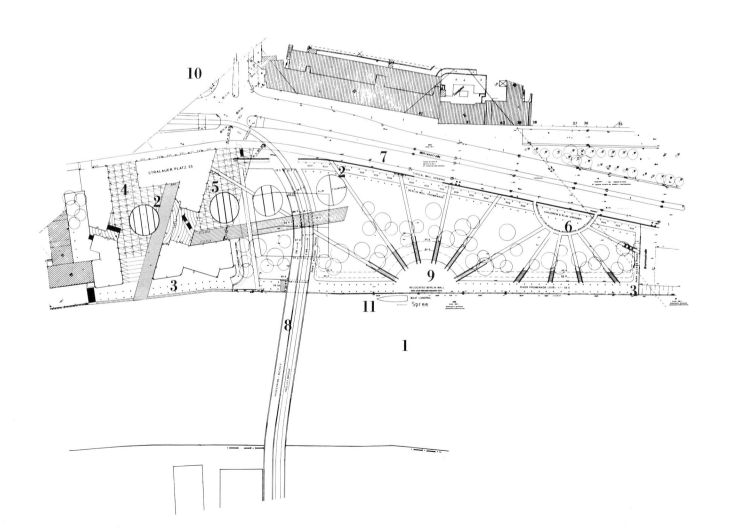

0   40 meters

is delineated by internal water fountains designed to form a unit in a progressive geometric sculpture. Granite boulders line the bottoms of the pools, reflecting lights from within and without as well as the building and sky.

The building atrium contains another stone terrace that flows outward as a porch toward the park, with its own dramatic stairway to access the river. An elegant paving pattern carpets the Winter Garden plaza with a vibrant mix of materials and colors. The 56-meter-high glass wall of the Winter Garden has a plaza scaled to allow informal cultural events.

The rejuvenation of Spree Park, a large open space of Berlin formerly adjacent to the desolate Berlin Wall, is an exciting component of the landscape plan.

Although much of the Wall is now gone, this park preserves a remaining 250-meter segment as a commemorative gesture to Berlin's recent divisive history. A section of the Wall will be relocated across the park to the riverfront, where it will serve as the focal point of cross axes. These will be in the form of two adjoining and opposing sunburst rays, transversing the park and connecting all areas while also forming a series of individual spaces with specific features and functions (children's playground, playing fields, etc.).

The park is experienced linearly, extending through spaces cut in the remains of the Wall to the River Spree with its broad promenade and a view of the city to the west. Within the design is a gradual slope of the rolling lawn leading visually and actually to the riverfront promenade. Seating in sun and shade, a raised viewing bank along the river, and a meeting space at the river's edge are included to make a functional, beautiful, and meaningful commemorative park. Offering a focal point for personal and public memory, the park of the Berlin Wall is a powerful symbol of the evolution of twentieth-century history.

The park will offer elements of healing and inspiration. Paintings and drawings left on the Wall will serve as a historic art gallery, allowing the eloquent personal markings to voice the feelings of the people whose lives were so intricately altered by the Wall and the political climate that generated it.

The riverside also accommodates a recreational boat landing along the esplanade's seawall. The esplanade is envisioned as a tree-lined and lighted colonnade that can be extended in both directions along the river. Richly paved in crushed stone, the esplanade affords a view of the upper reaches of the park and the flowing river.

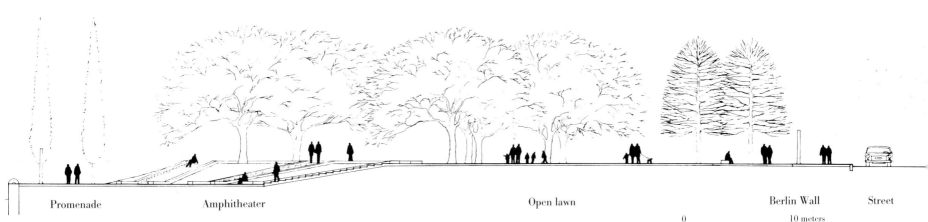

Promenade   Amphitheater   Open lawn   Berlin Wall   Street

0   10 meters

Cross section through park

Sitting area

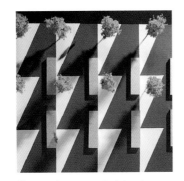

Geometric stone mosaic paving, tree grid, and benches

Stainless steel and glass bench illuminated from within

173

21st Century Tower and Plaza

Location: *Shanghai, China*
Client: *Shanghai 21st Century Center Real Estate Co., Ltd.*
Architect: *Murphy/Jahn, Inc., Architects*
Landscape
Architect: *Peter Walker William Johnson and Partners*
Proposal: *1994*

1 Parking
2 Lobby
3 Entry walk
4 Bank
5 Plaza
6 Ramp
7 Drop-off
8 Street

0   12 meters

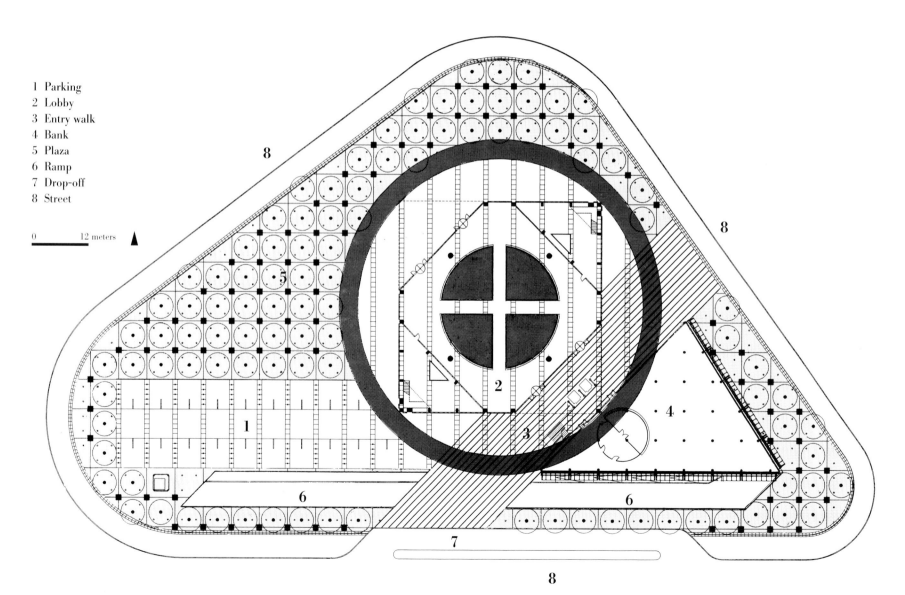

An essential geometry is at the heart of the design for the interior plaza and exterior level of the proposed Murphy/Jahn 21st Century Tower and Plaza in Shanghai, China. Intermingling with the simplicity of the geometry, a perceived element of surrealism adds dimension and intrigue to the design. Conceived in concert with the proportion, materials, and surface finish of the building, the landscape scheme envisions the plaza as a sculptural base to the tower, a relationship further emphasized by the grand scale of the urban street grid that surrounds it.

Within the motif of a large radius encircling the base of the structure, the plan creates a collage in varying textures and hues. The tower and interior plaza level rest on a circle of white stone stripes extending from exterior to interior areas, further delineated at the edge by a wide path of midnight gray cobblestones.

A series of narrow metal bands overlay diagonally through the other pavements at an automobile entrance, integrating the space of the tower lobby entrance with an adjacent structure. The plaza paving is a series of perforated aluminum modules that integrate and play off other grids of the plan. As if enlivening the corners and edges, square, black, matte-finish granite benches are sited to accentuate as well as to deconstruct the geometric forms. These offer a realm of eccentric possibilities for relating natural and fabricated elements, subtly drawing visitors' attention to unusual spatial perceptions. The perforated paving modules ground a series of dawn redwood trees and white metal bollards that either rest on or emerge through the pavement creating, in effect, an exotic continuous grove. The trunks of the living trees are painted white to mirror the profile of the painted bollards, shaping a visual density of human-scale verticality. The relationship of trees and poles, often seen and used but rarely magnified, expresses a sharp awareness of the specific space and structure of the multilevel project, focusing the visitors on their own standing form as participants in the design.

A ramp parapet leads to parking below. Another parking area on the plaza level is designed as part of the collage of patterns, this one covered in warm gray cobble alternating with white stone stripes. The plaza-level parking also contains white metal bollards as a design echo, functional delineation of the individual parking stalls, and extension of the urban orchard experience.

Bicycle locking bollards and orchard grids

Stone benches and bollards

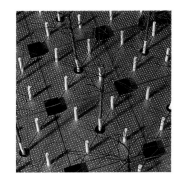

Cast metal panel paving with white bollards

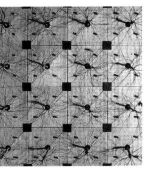

Cast aluminum reflective paving

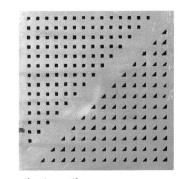

Aluminum tile

Oyama Training Center

Location: Oyama, Tochigi Prefecture, Japan
Client: Tokio Marine and Fire Insurance Co., Ltd.
Architect: Kunihide Oshinomi, Kajima Design
Landscape
Architect: Peter Walker William Johnson and Partners
Completed: 1995

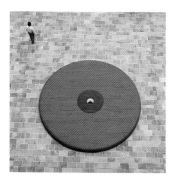

Wood disk with central light

1 Training Center
2 Castle garden
3 Parking
4 Entry
5 Auditorium
6 "Farm" garden
7 Poplar hedgerow
8 Hedge

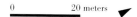

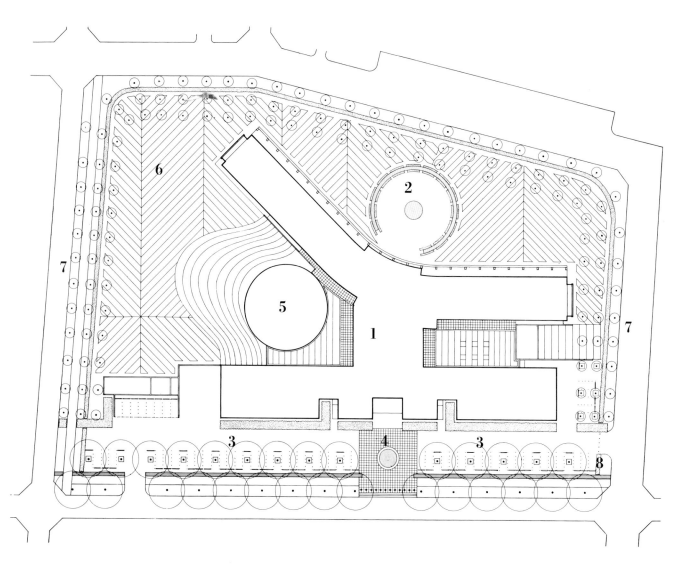

Located on the outskirts of Tokyo, the Oyama Training Center is sited in a historically agricultural area. The architectural design by Kunihide Oshinomi of Kajima Design in collaboration with the garden design of Peter Walker William Johnson and Partners creates a literal oasis that recalls the agricultural past amid the urban landscape of the current city. Formed by two attached buildings, the plan composites the refined lines of a main structure in spatial dialogue with the sweep of a curvilinear wing, which serves as a metaphor for a barn with a curved form and roof. These structures provide both a link with cultural history and a manifestation of modern architectural concept.

The Walker design demonstrates connections between many of the disciplines and historical threads that have inspired his work. Certainly, the differentiated sections within the landscape design indicate a direct relationship to a view of cultivated fields from above. The patterns of this garden offer a familiar image of an overlay of the purposeful marks of the farmer on the natural landscape. The internal patterns of various "fields" of the garden, composed of grasses and gravels, contain individual and distinct order in striped, zigzag, and radiating patterns that reflect both ancient decorative motifs and the contemporary paintings by artists such as Frank Stella, Alfred Jensen, and Jasper Johns, for example.

Walker has infused this generalized sequence with a collection of accessible and yet mysterious garden components to inhabit the overall pattern and to make the gardens livable as well as viewable.

Conceived as a villa-garden for the Training Center, the plan offers a triple allée of poplar trees that surround the site, allowing private walkways that both separate the Center from the community and provide glimpses from one to the other.

The arrival courtyard is marked with a large wooden disk of carved timbers lying on a square plane of slate that is delineated by a square of light. This bright red sculptural disk reveals a central cutout hole from which a deep violet light emanates. In another area, a double curved row of pruned hedges creates an

open yet protected circular space with a half-hidden pool between the hedges and a fountain at its center.

The Tokio Marine Oyama Training Center is a distinguished example of Walker's ability to synthesize the conceptual and functional values of a garden, while responding to the strength and poetry of the architecture and the unique qualities of the environmental situation.

Planting the grasses

Grass and gravel grid

Spring

Summer grass

Fall

Castle garden with pool between hedges

Castle garden with central fountain and hedges

New England Aquarium

Location: Boston, Massachusetts
Client: New England Aquarium
Architect: Schwartz Silver and Associates
Landscape
Architect: Peter Walker William Johnson and Partners
Projected
completion: 2004

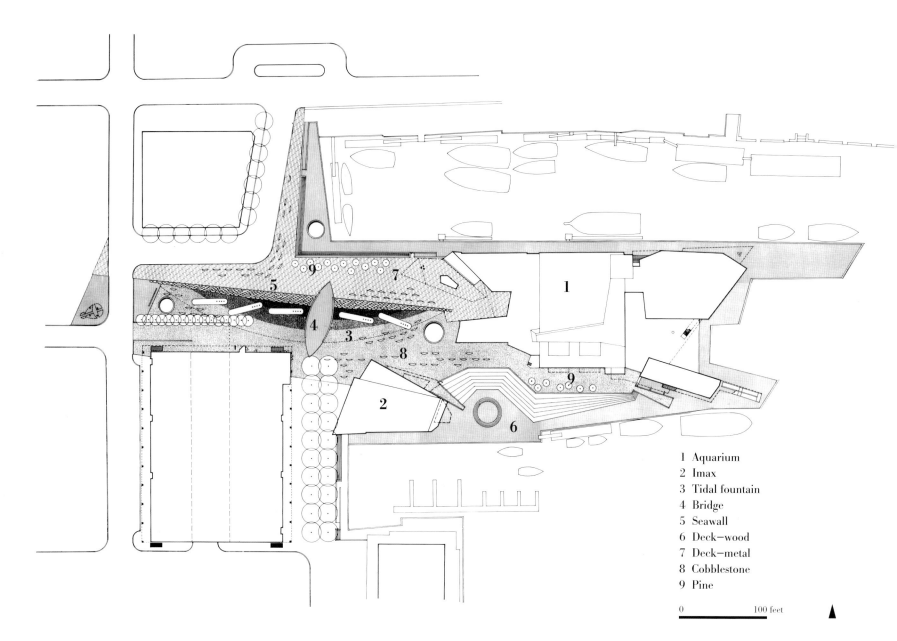

1 Aquarium
2 Imax
3 Tidal fountain
4 Bridge
5 Seawall
6 Deck—wood
7 Deck—metal
8 Cobblestone
9 Pine

0   100 feet

The New England Aquarium plaza is a public commission in which Peter Walker William Johnson and Partners anticipates and concentrates the experience of wonder for visitors to the aquarium.

On the edge of Boston Harbor in proximity to other popular public sites, including Faneuil Hall and the Holocaust Memorial, the contextual environment is one heavily trafficked by people from around the world.

The space responds inventively to the various needs required of a public plaza: the outside "deck" area for the gathering of large crowds reflects the themes of imaginary boats, abstracted whales, and metaphoric illusions to adventures of the sea while still providing places for intimate discovery, engagement, rest, and play. The plaza here extends the experience of the aquarium in perhaps the most narrative and interactive of all of the firm's recent work. Movement on the metal surface paving evokes the sound of footsteps on a modern ship deck, while a wooden walkway stretching to the harbor suggests seafaring vessels of an earlier era. Fountain pools with time-regulated tides that gently flood and then recede, spray around dark islands that replicate fantastic marine mammals and submarines. A seawall of granite marks and defines the animation at the water's edge. Bridges in open areas and aluminum tubes with spouting water add to the imaginative experience, as do portholelike windows in the deck that allow a glimpse of the exhibitions and underworld below.

The design offers a midpoint transition from the more everyday world to the wonders and mysteries of nature that the aquarium personifies.

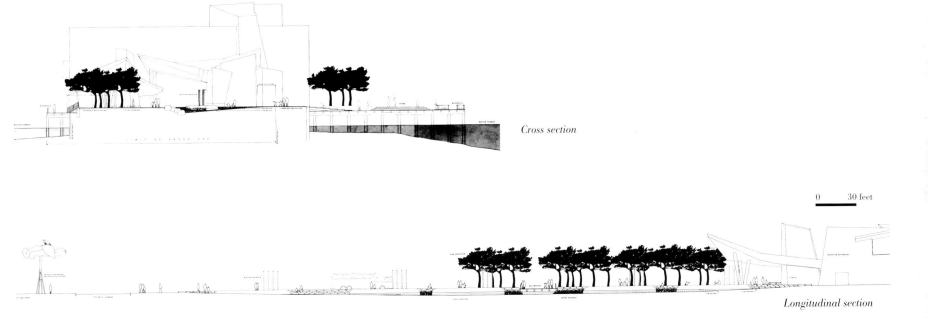

Cross section

0   30 feet

Longitudinal section

Belgian block cobblestones

Wood deck

Metal deck

Sony Center Berlin

Location: Berlin, Germany
Client: Sony Corporation
Architect: Murphy/Jahn, Inc., Architects
Engineer: Ove Arup & Partners
Landscape
Architect: Peter Walker William Johnson and Partners
Projected
completion: 2000

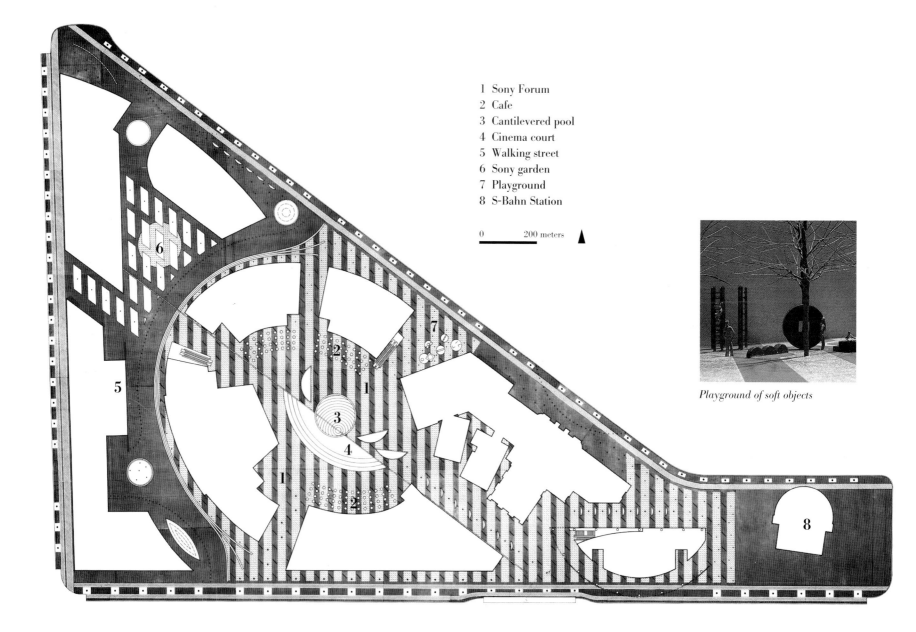

1 Sony Forum
2 Cafe
3 Cantilevered pool
4 Cinema court
5 Walking street
6 Sony garden
7 Playground
8 S-Bahn Station

0   200 meters

Playground of soft objects

Resulting from one of the early competitions in Berlin after the fall of the Berlin Wall, the winning design by Murphy/Jahn, Inc., Architects and Peter Walker William Johnson and Partners for Sony Berlin Center offered many unique physical and conceptual challenges in helping to define and enunciate the physical visage of the new, free Berlin. In addition to the poignant and powerful political context, Berlin continues to be acknowledged as a characteristically distinct European city recognized for its cultural individuality, as a locus for the arts and ideas, and as a historical gathering space.

Sited near Potsdamer Platz, Sony Berlin Center was conceived in the collaborative plan of Helmut Jahn and Peter Walker as a twenty-first-century model for a town square in a modern and urban scale. Nevertheless, references to Berlin's unique historic, physical, and cultural identity are carefully integrated in the plan.

Covered by an enormous, cable-suspended glass and steel tent, with open air entrances to the cobblestoned streets and sidewalks on three sides, the center is initially defined by a floor of striped paving that continues the traditional cobbles of Berlin, alternating them with a fabricated aluminum paving. This new metal paving reveals its own interior pattern of lustrous alternating lines, reiterating the vitality and dimension of rhythm.

In another extension of the exterior street with the new interior plaza, linden trees (traditional to Berlin's tree-lined streets) are placed linearly along the boulevard, in the plaza, and within the design of the metal and cobblestone paving. Irregular plantings extend the north side into the existing Tiergarten. (A technically advanced substructure below the paved floors allows for dirt-fill materials and drainage beneath the surface of the design.)

A predominant ingredient in the central plaza design is a framing of the relationship between the lower and plaza levels, expressed with an abstract, constructivist-inspired composition. Using the overlapping forms and spaces of the three-dimensional, kinetic work of artists related to Bauhaus ideas, including Naum Gabo and László Moholy-Nagy, Walker's dynamic design connects the two floors through a large crescent-shaped opening almost at the centerpoint of the space. Extending from the plaza floor into the cutout crescent is a circular pool, cantilevered over the opening in a duplicating curve. A graduated three-layer arced hedge ripples out from the pool. Three moon-shaped arcs, outlined in stainless steel and planted with flowers in single primary colors, orbit the central pool. The movement of this composition ultimately turns on a lighted glass line that connects and dissects the composition. This centerpiece work, surrounded by cafes, is seen from above.

With directions and dimensions seeming to change at every angle of vision depending on the point of view of people moving through the space, this enlivened, monumental, three-dimensional relief offers perspectives reaching back to the roots of modern German design and into the twenty-first century.

Constructivist garden with cantilevered pool

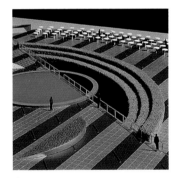

Opening to cinema court

View from lower cinema courtyard

Bench, stepping hedges, and pool

Metal panel and stone mosaic paving with diagonal lights

Metal hedges with ivy

Cafes on metal and stone mosaic paving

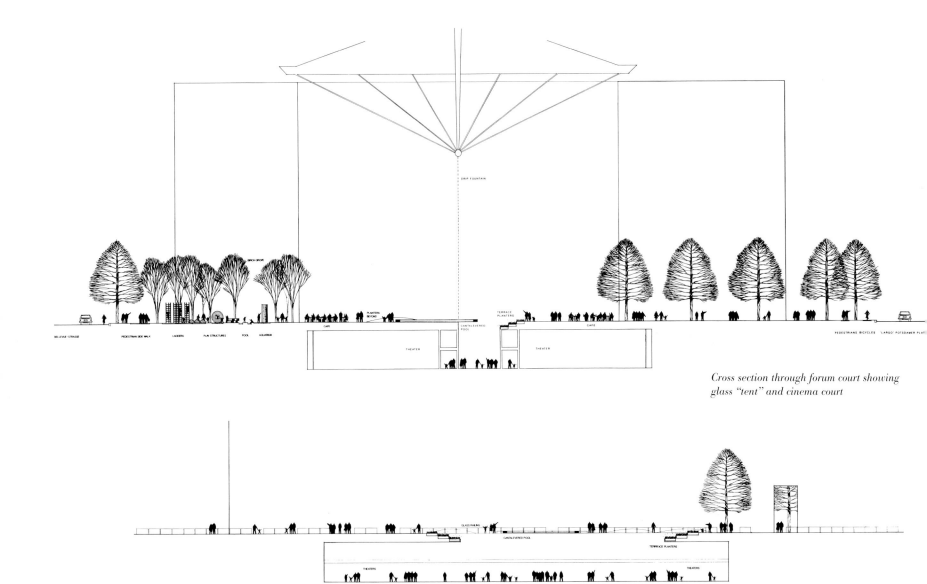

Cross section through forum court showing glass "tent" and cinema court

Longitudinal section showing illuminated glass rail and cinema court

0   7 meters

Industrial & Commercial Bank of China

Location: *Beijing, China*
Client: *Industrial & Commercial Bank of China*
Architect: *Skidmore, Owings & Merrill, Architects*
Landscape
Architect: *Peter Walker William Johnson and Partners*
Project
completion: *1998*

Based upon an ancient concept of a city's heart as the circular central form within a square protective wall, Peter Walker William Johnson and Partners' garden for the Industrial & Commercial Bank of China in Beijing echoes the structure by Skidmore, Owings & Merrill. Framed by small, ornately patterned corner bamboo gardens of black and white stone, the dominant form of the design lies in an extraordinary, 360-foot-diameter circle of rich red poppies (encircled by red, low clipped hedges), which serves both as flat solid form and as active volume of color when the poppies sway on their stems in the wind. This intense device transforms the space, illuminating our awareness and perception of what the circle is and can be. The red mass personifies the unique qualities and possibilities of landscape art as it changes with the seasons, incorporating the balance of the artistic concept and vision with the ultimately unpredictable events and effects of nature. This uneasy and essential collaboration is at the crux of the risk, promise, and excitement of landscape art.

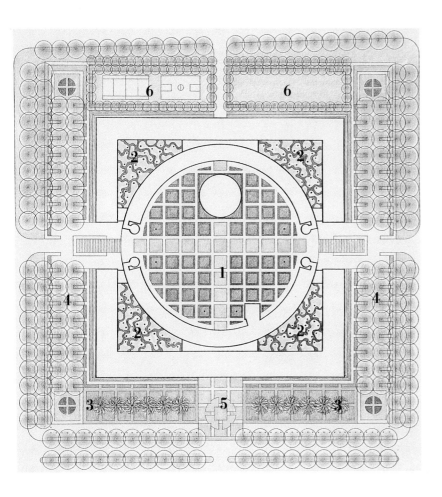

1 Red circular parterre
2 Black and white bamboo gardens
3 Entry water gardens
4 Parking
5 Entrance plaza
6 Playgrounds

0   36 meters

Saitama Sky Forest Plaza

Location: *Saitama Prefecture, Japan*
Client: *Saitama Prefectural Government*
Design
Team: *Peter Walker William Johnson and Partners*
Ohtori Consultants
NTT Urban Development Co.

Projected
completion: *2000*

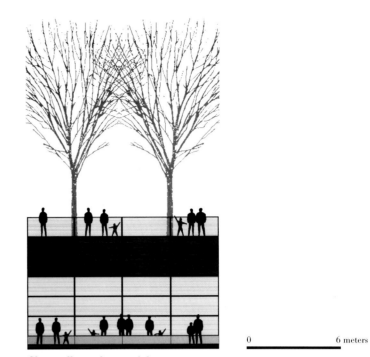

Glass wall revealing earth layer

0   6 meters

Hikawa Shrine

Plaza and grand stair to street level

1 Restaurant tower
2 Sunken plaza
3 Lawn
4 Escalator
5 Elevator
6 Fountain/cascade
7 Bench
8 Bridge

0   16 meters

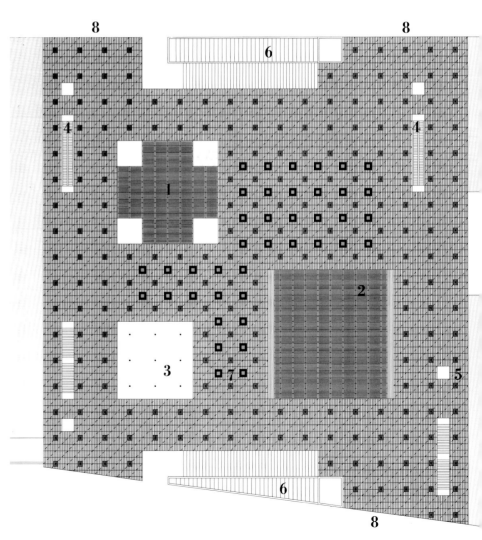

The Sky Forest for the Saitama Plaza represents an exciting scientific, technical, and artistic achievement. Responding to the intent of the new urban center and to its history, the core of the landscape concept revolves around the innovative application of technology to transplant and revision nature.

Saitama Plaza and the new Arena is the hub of a major urban plan for the Saitama New Downtown, site of a former railroad train yard at the convergence of three cities in the prefecture of Saitama, just north of Tokyo. Traditionally linked literally and spiritually to the revered Hikawa Shrine by the ancient tree-lined Zelkova Road, this New Downtown will serve to decentralize a number of transportation and government activities formerly focused in Tokyo, while creating a beautiful and highly self-sufficient urban district for the residents of the towns and prefecture. The plan offers a direct transit network linking the new center with Tokyo and other major cities, and is the site of relocation for seventeen government agencies currently based in Tokyo.

The Saitama Sky Forest is a large fabricated garden based on the idea of transporting a squared-off section of the earth, metaphorically and physically, and planting it in the heart of an urban web of multiuse infrastructure, a place that would otherwise seem totally disconnected from its cultural roots of viewing nature as an expression of life.

Composed of two main levels, street and the higher plaza level 27 feet above, the plan creates a kind of floating forest of more than two hundred zelkova trees supported by the formidable earthen slab of the central plaza garden. The edges of the massive square of earth are sheathed in specially tempered glass, allowing direct viewing of this improbable and unique agricultural system. A sophisticated ecologically advanced procedure utilizing hydroponic techniques to encourage urban tree growth and drainage was assembled especially for this project, serving as well to minimize plant disease.

Echoing the architectural columns of the grid structure supporting the plaza, the trunks of the dark zelkova trees grow out of a level, horizontal sheath of fabricated stainless steel tiles that form the geometric surface of the forest ground. Playing off the irony of the earthen chunk exposed from the sides, the metal "land surface" of the plaza's Sky Forest serves as a technological membrane cloaking the earth beneath with a luminous, reflective surface. To lighten the rhythm and enliven the space, an overlay of lights in a diagonal pattern is set below the ground tiles. Within the overall ground area of the plaza level, additional functional and compositional elements, including a sunken plaza paved in laminated concrete and glass panels, clear glass railings, and a series of wood and glass benches, increase the visual dynamic and provide places for corresponding activities in this operative urban space.

A system of ramps, stairs, elevators, and escalators connects the street and plaza levels, highlighted by a series of graduated, glass-bottomed streams flowing diagonally in between. Joined in visual metaphor, the new technology supports the traditional zelkova trees, referencing the relationship of modern society to the venerated past. The complexity of these old and new alliances is mirrored in the layered scale of the design, acknowledging each as a foundation of the spirit of place.

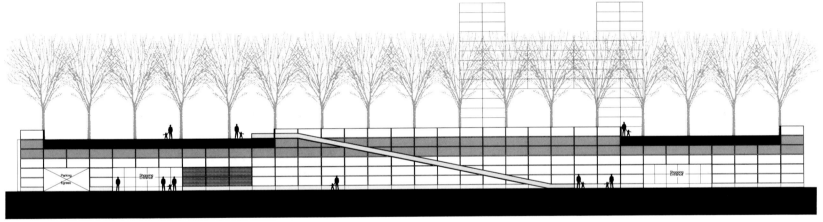

Elevation showing commercial and plaza levels and earth slab

0   6 meters

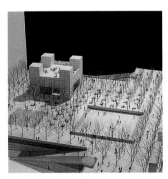

Sky Forest and restaurant tower

Grand stair

Lawn

Stainless steel grid pavement

Walker Memorial

Location: *Mendocino, California*
Designers: *Peter Walker and David Walker*
Meadow
Consultant: *John Greenlee*
Completed: *1995*

For their family's private memorial, Peter Walker and his son and partner David Walker created a stepped commemorative garden on a hillside overlooking the town of Mendocino, California. Sited near the family's weekend home, with forested hills in the background on the north side and the rugged California coast beyond the town's rooftops to the south and west, the Walker Memorial is designed to be visited as an intimate family spot: a place to walk to, linger at, and find a peaceful haven. Offering a space for private meditation within an existing historic cemetery, this is a thoughtfully cultivated and beautifully calm setting, revealing both metaphors for individual identity and a larger connection to the surrounding terrain, history, and community memory.

The memorial contains four long, low, rectangular concrete vaults, each composed of ten identical square units, capped with dark gray granite stone.

Functioning as both benches and surfaces on which to inscribe factual and personal information about memorialized family members, these long stone markers are installed in an equidistant sequence on the gentle hillside grade. Existing flora consists mostly of native plants, but the Walkers added complexity and depth by introducing a rich and unusual mix of flowers, grasses, and reeds.

The color red is prominent, with red poppies and rambling red roses growing around and over the angular, cool stones. Small meadows of wildflowers appear in between the benches, adding a lightness of mood, variety with the seasons, and also signifying recent visitors whose footsteps will temporarily matte the meadows.

The Walkers' care in choosing familiar and meaningful components ensures that the simple, profound intention of memory be expressed with grace.

*Stepped stone vaults
looking southeast*

View north

Carved stone bench

Biographies

Notes

Credits

Peter Walker

Peter Walker is a landscape architect with forty years of experience in practice and teaching. The scope of his concerns has varied, from the design and crafting of small gardens to the planning, design, and development of cities and extensive new communities. Much of his work and thought has been devoted to problems of a middle scale, however: academic campuses, corporate headquarters, civic and quasi-public plazas, and areas of urban revitalization. Throughout his varied work, he continues to search beyond merely functional solutions, to shape outdoor spaces that remain meaningful and memorable for the people who bring them to life.

Cofounder of the East Coast firm, Sasaki Walker and Associates (established 1957), Mr. Walker opened the firm's West Coast office, which became The SWA Group in 1975. As principal, consulting principal, and chairman of the board, he helped to shape The SWA Group as a multidisciplinary office with an international reputation for excellence in environmental design. In 1983 he formed a smaller office in order to work more personally with his clients.

Peter Walker has served as consultant and adviser to public agencies and institutions, such as the Redevelopment Agency of San Francisco, the Port Authority of San Diego, Stanford University, the Universities of Washington and California, and the American Academy in Rome. He formerly chaired the Department of Landscape Architecture and was Acting Director of the Urban Design Program at Harvard University's Graduate School of Design. He is a fellow of the American Society of Landscape Architects and the Institute for Urban Design. He has also received the American Institute of Architects' Institute Honor Award.

Projects in Japan, France, Germany, Spain, Mexico, the Philippines, and other countries have allowed Mr. Walker, his partners, and staff to test their ideas on urbanism and environmental design in a range of geographical and cultural climates.

Mr. Walker and his firm have won numerous design competitions including the redesign of Todos Santos Plaza in downtown Concord, California; the urban renewal Martin Luther King, Jr., Promenade, in San Diego; the Cultural Arts Center in Fremont, California, with BOOR/A Architects; the Federal Triangle in Washington, D.C., with I. M. Pei Architects; the Clark County, Nevada, Government Center with C. W. Fentress, J. H. Bradburn Architects, and Civitas, Landscape Architects; the Sony Center Berlin with Murphy/Jahn, Inc., Architects; the T. F. Green Airport Public Art Competition with Ned Kahn, artist; and the Commercial & Industrial Bank of China with Skidmore, Owings & Merrill Architects. The firm was also a member of the only American team to be a finalist in a competition to extend the Great Axis of Paris to the west of La Défense.

Peter Walker has coauthored a book titled *Invisible Gardens: The Search for Modernism in the American Landscape*, which traces the history of modern landscape architecture in the United States.

Education

Harvard University Graduate School of Design; Master of Landscape Architecture, 1957; Weidenman Prize, 1957

University of Illinois; Graduate Study in Landscape Architecture, 1956

University of California at Berkeley; Bachelor of Science in Landscape Architecture, 1955

Professional Experience

Peter Walker William Johnson and Partners, Landscape Architecture

Peter Walker and Partners

The Office of Peter Walker and Martha Schwartz

The SWA Group

Sasaki Walker and Associates

Hideo Sasaki & Associates

Landscape Architects Associates

Lawrence Halprin and Associates Landscape Architects

Teaching Experience

Regent Professor, University of California at Berkeley, 1996

Charles Eliot Chair, Harvard University Graduate School of Design, 1992

Adjunct Professor, Harvard University Graduate School of Design, 1976–1991

Chairman, Department of Landscape Architecture, Harvard University Graduate School of Design, 1978–1981

Acting Director, Urban Design Program, Harvard University Graduate School of Design, 1977–1978

Director, SWA Group Summer Program, 1973–1983

Visiting Critic, Massachusetts Institute of Technology, 1959

Instructor in Landscape Architecture, Harvard University Graduate School of Design, 1958–1959

Guest Lecturer/Visiting Critic:
University of California at Berkeley
University of California at Davis
Washington University
University of Washington
University of Virginia
Louisiana State University
Ohio State University
University of Colorado
University of Illinois
Pennsylvania State University
University of Massachusetts
University of Michigan
University of New Mexico
Universidad Menendez-Pelayo
Collegi D'Arquitectes de Catalunya
Rapperswile Summer Academy, Switzerland

Speaker:
The Jerusalem Seminar in Architecture, Israel, 1996
Wave Hill, New York, 1995
California Center for the Arts Museum, Escondido, California, 1995
XXXI World Congress, IFLA, Mexico, 1994
Third International Symposium of Architects, Mexico, 1994
Monterey Design Conference, 1993
Municipal Art Society, New York City, 1992
Singapore, 1991
Kajima/Harvard Graduate School of Design Conference, Tokyo, Japan, 1989
IFLA, Boston, 1988

Registration

CLARB Certification
Landscape Architect: California, Florida, Georgia, Illinois, Maryland, Massachusetts, Michigan, Nebraska, New York, North Carolina, Pennsylvania, Oregon, and Texas

Honors

American Institute of Architects, Institute Honor 1992

Resident, American Academy in Rome, 1991

Fellow, American Society of Landscape Architects

Fellow, Institute for Urban Design

Editorial Board, *Landscape Architecture*, 1988–1991

Winning Entries:
Saitama Plaza, Saitama
Prefecture, Japan, 1995
Industrial & Commercial Bank of China, Beijing, 1993
T. F. Green Airport, Rhode Island, 1993
Sony Center Berlin, 1992
Clark County Administration Complex, Nevada, 1992
Federal Triangle, Washington, D.C., 1990
Fremont Performing Arts Center, Fremont, California, 1988
San Diego Marina Linear Park, San Diego, California, 1988
Todos Santos Plaza Competition, City of Concord and National Endowment for the Arts, 1987

Design Juries:
American Institute of Architects
American Society of Landscape Architects
Prince of Wales Prize in Urban Design
American Academy in Rome, Landscape Architecture
National Endowment for the Arts, First Collaborative Awards Jury
Progressive Architecture Urban Design Awards
National Building Museum Honor Awards

Awards

Federal Housing Authority
American Society of Landscape Architects
American Institute of Architects
American Institute of Planning
New York Architectural League
San Francisco Gold Balloon
National Endowment for the Arts

Publications

Landscape Architecture
Architectural Record
Architectural Forum
Progressive Architecture
Modern Gardens—Avant Garde, Museum of Modern Art
Arts and Architecture
domus, Italy
SD Magazine, Japan

Process: Architecture, Japan
Architectural Review, England
MASS Shinkenchiku, Japan
L' ARCA, Italy
Lotus, Italy
Global Architecture, Japan
Six Views, Contemporary Landscape Architecture
Avant Garde
Sculpture
Quaderns, Spain
Garten + Landschaft 1,
Arch +, Germany
Pages Paysages, France
Japan Landscape, Japan
Shinkenchiku, Japan
Graphis, New York

Book

Invisible Gardens: The Search for Modernism in the American Landscape, with Melanie Simo, MIT Press, 1994.

Exhibitions

"California: In Three Dimensions," California Center for the Arts Museum, Escondido, California, 1995. Catalogue

"The Way of Collaboration: The Landscape Architecture of Peter Walker William Johnson and Partners in Collaborative Work with Architects Arata Isozaki, Helmut Jahn, Ricardo Legorreta, Kunihide Oshinomi (Kajima Design), Skidmore, Owings & Merrill, Yoshio Taniguchi," Yamagiwa Roppongi Inspiration Gallery, Tokyo, Japan, 1993. Catalogue

"Peter Walker and Partners: Landscape Architecture: Recent Work," Jernigan Wicker Gallery, San Francisco, California, 1992

"Landscape as Art," Corcoran Gallery of Art, Washington, D.C., 1992

"Manifeste: Selections from the Permanent Collection of the Centre Georges Pompidou," Centre Georges Pompidou, Paris, France, 1992

Leah Levy

Leah Levy is an independent art curator and writer living in Berkeley, California. She studied the history of art at Simmons College and Tufts University in Massachusetts, and was the director of the Parker Street 470 Gallery, the seminal Boston gallery of large-scale painting and sculpture, in the early 1970s. From 1974 to 1983 she owned and directed the Leah Levy Gallery in San Francisco. As founding curator of Capp Street Project, the internationally recognized artist-in-residency program in San Francisco, she worked with artists including James Turrell, David Ireland, and Mary Lucier. In 1989 she was appointed Trustee of the Estate of the artist Jay DeFeo.

Ms. Levy's previous work with the landscapes of Peter Walker includes organizing the 1993 Tokyo exhibition "The Way of Collaboration: The Landscape Architecture of Peter Walker William Johnson and Partners in Collaborative Work with Architects Arata Isozaki, Helmut Jahn, Ricardo Legorreta, Kunihide Oshinomi (Kajima Design), Skidmore, Owings & Merrill, Yoshio Taniguchi," for which she contributed an essay and edited the catalogue.

Sarah Vance

Sarah Vance is a graphic design consultant and landscape architect in Cambridge, Massachusetts. From 1976 to 1985 she was a partner at The GNU Group, a marketing communications firm in Sausalito, California, where clients included several landscape architecture and architecture firms.

The catalyst for the first American Society of Landscape Architects (ASLA) marketing competition, Ms. Vance served as a juror in 1993 and 1994. She was a juror for the Boston Society of Landscape Architecture (BSLA) awards program in 1994. Her graphic design has been recognized by several organizations and publications, including the American Institute of Graphic Arts, the Presidential Awards of the National Endowment for the Arts, *Graphis*, *Time*, and the BSLA.

Ms. Vance is on the landscape design faculty at the Radcliffe Seminars. She was a visiting critic at the Rhode Island School of Design in 1993. She received a Bachelor of Fine Arts in graphic design from the University of Arizona, and a Master of Landscape Architecture with Distinction from the Harvard University Graduate School of Design, where she was awarded the Weidenman Prize.

Notes

1. Peter Walker and Melanie Simo, *Invisible Gardens: The Search for Modernism in the American Landscape* (Cambridge: Massachusetts Institute of Technology Press, 1994).
2. Frances Colpitt, *Minimal Art: The Critical Perspective* (Seattle: University of Washington Press, 1993).
3. Maurice Tuchman et al., *The Spiritual in Art: Abstract Painting, 1890–1985* (New York: Abbeville Press, 1986).
4. John Beardsley, *Earthworks and Beyond: Contemporary Art in the Landscape* (New York: Abbeville Press, 1989).

Photography Credits

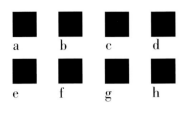

a b c d
e f g h

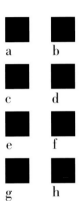

a b
c d
e f
g h

Tom Adams
38, 125g

Gerry Campbell
14–15, 16, 28–29, 31, 32, 33, 121efg, 123adfg

Dixi Carrillo
12, 13, 24, 47, 48, 49, 50, 51, 53c, 62, 63, 64, 65, 67b, 106, 107, 115, 129bcdfgh, 131ac, 136, 137abcd, 140, 141bde, 147h, 151cdf, 155abcd, 161abcd, 167abef, 171abcdef, 173abc, 175acdgh, 181e, 185d

Geoffrey Clements
20

Doug Findlay
167c

Tom Fox
37, 125f

Gian Franco Gorgoni
21

Tim Harvey
82–83, 84, 112, 113, 114, 116–117, 157bdef, 180, 181abcdfg, 184c, 185abc

Jim Hedrich
6, 46, 52, 129a

Susumu Koshimizu
79b, 79d, 149dh

Tom Leader
86, 155ef

David Meyer
58, 85, 135g, 157ac, 161efg

Hiko Mitani
88, 89, 90, 92, 93, 94, 95, 103, 108, 110A, 158ab, 159abcdfgh, 163abcdeg, 165fg 177ab

Murphy/Jahn, Inc., Architects
Engelhardt/Sellin, Photographers
Aschau I.CH., Germany
72, 73, 145abc, 172

Atsushi Nakamichi
96–97, 99, 100, 101, 163fh, 164a, 165acde

Pamela Palmer
66, 67a, 67c, 67d, 79a, 81, 98, 102, 104, 141fg, 143f, 146, 147d, 149acf, 156, 164b, 165bh, 169a

Raymond Rajaonarivelo
168abcd

Yoji Sasaki
184

Yutaka Shinozawa
111, 176

Tony Sinkosky
143dh

David Walker
11, 30, 40, 41, 42, 43, 44, 53a, 53b, 53d, 54, 55, 56–57, 59, 60, 110b, 110c, 123c, 127abcdfgh, 130ce, 131e, 133cefgh, 135abch, 141a, 169b, 177cfh, 179bc

Peter Walker
18, 19, 23, 74, 75, 76, 78, 79c, 80, 91, 109, 110d, 124, 133a, 143a, 145defgh, 149beg, 159e, 172b, 177eg, 179a, 186abc

Alan Ward
26, 27, 34, 35, 36, 39, 120abdefh, 125abceh

James Wilson
130a

Eiji Yonekura
68–69, 70, 71, 143bceg

Gerry Zekowski
161h

Drawings

William Johnson
118, 138ef, 139def, 153abgh, 162a

Translations

Los Paisajes de Peter Walker

Leah Levy

Nuestra categorización contemporánea del paisaje creado se asocia de manera consistente y específica, más directamente con la arquitectura. En ese contexto, el "arquitecto" del paisaje ha sido típicamente relegado a planificador de los espacios alrededor de, y entre, las estructuras del arquitecto, que son los monumentos más discerniblemente visibles en el paisaje. En las universidades contemporáneas, las disciplinas de arquitectura y arquitectura del paisaje comparten los mismos departamentos, habiendo sido trasladada la arquitectura del paisaje de su anterior asociación con escuelas de agricultura y horticultura. Críticamente, los vocabularios tradicionales para el discurso acerca del paisaje y jardines diseñados son aquellos destinados para la arquitectura o agricultura.

Al considerar la obra del arquitecto del paisaje, Peter Walker, los criterios convencionales de evaluación de la arquitectura del paisaje y los jardines, son limitantes. Aunque la obra madura de Walker se ha enfocado a la "visibilidad" del paisaje a través del diseño, generando su propuesta del campo como una entidad independiente con un lugar y condición adecuados a las artes visuales, el arte teatral y la arquitectura; la literatura crítica actual sobre el paisaje creado es notablemente escasa, en comparación con la de las otras artes.

Los indicadores del estilo de Walker se pueden rastrear hacia fuentes diferentes y, sin embargo, lógicamente relacionadas. Vestigios arquetípicos y primitivos sobre la tierra como las Líneas de Nazca en Perú o Stonehenge en Inglaterra, demuestran un impulso básico y comunal de marcar la tierra. En gran parte de la obra de Walker, se manifiesta una apremiante necesidad básica humana de comunicarse con el grandioso medio ambiente, de indicar una consciencia y una búsqueda de la conexión con misterios terrenales y celestiales, así como de aludir al poder de las fuerzas superiores. Existen muchos casos en donde la obra se enfoca a las cualidades enigmáticas de la naturaleza, representadas por el sonido del agua, la estasis y peso de la piedra, los cambios susurrantes del viento, bloques y diseños de colores cambiantes, brumas mágicas y brillantes, así como la luz esquiva.

En un contexto similar, el orden clásico de los jardines franceses del siglo XVII, especialmente aquellos de Andre Le Nôtre, sientan un fuerte precedente para los elementos individuales de la propuesta de Walker. Su afinidad, tanto intuitiva como intelectual a los diseños, los ritmos y el orden así como a un especie de síntesis cartesiana, se manifiesta a lo largo de su obra.

La influencia de jardines Zen, también se manifiesta con fuerza en la obra de Walker. Una destilación filosófica subyacenete de lo complejo para lograr lo simple, se evidencia tanto en componentes precisos como en la totalidad unificadora de muchos de sus jardines.

La obra de Walker también tiene sus raíces en la progresión de la historia del paisaje moderno. Como individuo, él está firmemente comprometido a ilustrar y rendir homenaje a la historia del diseño del paisaje de su siglo.[1] La obra de los creadores de jardines de mediados del siglo XX, especialmente Thomas Church e Isamu Noguchi, fueron particularmente una fuente de inspiración para Walker durante sus años de formación. Sin embargo, para refleccionar de manera eficaz sobre el éxito y significado de los paisajes de Walker, su lugar en la cultura contemporánea y el diálogo permanente entre su pensamiento y su obra con el arte, un análisis de los acontecimientos artísticos más importantes del siglo XX sería tal vez, el enfoque más pertinente y productivo con el propósito de ver su obra en un contexto cultural actual.

Las primeras décadas del siglo XX estuvieron repletas de innovaciones en el arte, la ciencia y la cultura, que habrían de dictar los rumbos de la investigación a lo largo del siglo. La iniciación de la abstracción pura en las artes visuales se encontraba centrada hacia una nueva percepción; esto es, un arte que no imitaba ni se refería a ninguna imagen real o física, sino que en su propia forma independiente y abstracta, servía como el medio perfecto de expresión y exploración. Tomando como base lo geométrico en mucha de esta original obra, especialmente la de los primeros constructivistas rusos, existía una lucha para acercarse, dar a conocer y retratar los misterios universales que la humanidad ha buscado a lo largo de la historia: las formas de considerar y comprender los fenómenos que experimentamos pero que no pueden ser explicados a través de representaciones tradicionales de la realidad.

Al liberar al arte bidimensional y tridimensional de restricciones de representación, se pudo así, aproximársele como por ejemplo a la música, como una experiencia independiente, sin la intención de reproducir una experiencia específica reconocible y con una nueva libertad para el artista y el observador de abrirse a reacciones a un nivel más allá del consciente.

Otro ejemplo del espíritu creativo de principios del siglo XX, fue la obra del artista francés Marcel Duchamp, quien rechazó el objeto (literal o abstracto) por su belleza o significado y extendió el ámbito del artista hasta un arte de la mente no-retinal. Duchamp exigía, para el artista, el derecho a determinar lo que pudiera considerarse arte, ampliando él campo para el análisis artístico. Desdibujando los limites de las categorías artísticas y confiriendo la condición de arte a cualquier objeto e idea que no pareciera arte que el escogiera, Duchamp creó opciones para los artistas, más allá de las tradiciones de la pintura y la escultura, que se siguen explorando y que marcan el rumbo a mucha de la investigación artística en nuestros días.

Junto con influencias sociales, políticas y culturales, los avances de los abstraccionistas, como así también las prácticas del arte conceptual de Duchamp parecieran haber convergido a mediados de siglo para formar las raíces históricas de lo que conocemos como "arte minimalista." Desde sus años más cruciales en la década de los años sesenta, el minimalismo, discutiblemente el primer arte verdaderamente norteamericano, se ha transformado en un término abarcativo, utilizado con ligereza, que ha sido absorbido en la cultura para referirse a estilos que son no-figurativos, no-referenciales, geométricos o meramente de pocas y simples partes.

Sin embargo, el término arte minimalista fue creado para identificar y referirse a un punto muy específico en el tiempo, aproximadamente 1963-1968, y a un pequeño grupo de artistas privados que trabajaban principalmente en la ciudad de Nueva York, incluyendo a Donald Judd, Dan Flavin, Sol Le Witt, Robert Morris y Carl Andre. La obra de estos artistas refleja una base filosófica que rechazaba los intentos de clasificación tradicional: la intención principal del artista era crear objetos que ocuparan espacio y que fueran percibidos en proximidad física con el propio cuerpo del espectador, quien a su vez, estaría ocupando un espacio[2], en una "comunicación irreproducible".[3]

Los materiales como objetos en el espacio fueron el sujeto y contenido del arte minimalista y era necesario que el espectador los percibiera en forma directa y los experimentara físicamente. Con la finalidad de llegar a la forma más directa de hacer que el objeto primario produjera una experiencia primaria, los artistas minimalistas buscaron un método y un resultado reductivos.

Debido a que el "contenido" del arte era la relación del objeto y el entorno con el espectador, estas obras eran consideradas a menudo, casi en última instancia, "formalistas": podían describirse bien (tamaño, forma, color), pero no podían explicarse sin la experiencia auténtica de caminar a su alrededor, a través de ellas, cerca de ellas y en ellas. En un orden abierto de características formales de estas obras, estaba incluido el uso de formas simples y geométricas, la repetición y la colocación sistematica de los objetos, el uso de materiales modernos y la fabricación industrial, las tres dimensiones (aunque significa un desafío el ser percibidas como esculturales), los colores primarios y la colocación de estructuras directamente sobre los pisos, apoyadas en las paredes y con relaciones inmediatas al espacio, sin pedestales ni armazón.

Otra característica importante de las obras de este período de arte minimalista se refiere a los espacios en los que se colocaban y se observaban, ya fuera en el "cubo blanco" de la galería o al aire libre. La escala relativa de todos los elementos era, frecuentemente, considerada y calculada de manera cuidadosa ya que su propósito era indicar las relaciones físicas y fenomenológicas entre los objetos, el cuerpo humano y el espacio en el que estos se situaban.

En tanto que el trabajo de Peter Walker comparte la sensibilidad de la estética formalista demostrada en la obra de los artistas minimalistas, éste también parece tener relaciones igualmente intensas con otros grupos de artistas del siglo XX. Estos artistas, cuyas obras pueden tener un aire de abstracción formalista sistemática que ha sido incluida en el término "minimalismo", crean su obra artística teniendo una premisa filosófica totalmente diferente. Incluyendo tanto a pintores como a creadores de objetos, artistas tales como Ad Reinhardt, Agnes Martin, Robert Ryman, Robert Mangold, Ellsworth Kelly, Porfirio DiDonna, Yves Klein, Jasper Johns, Robert Irwin, alinearon sus abstracciones con una búsqueda y un significado más subliminales. En algunas de estas obras, los ritmos y los diseños repetidos se refieren a los sistemas de organismos y a la cadencia de la poesía (la naturaleza repetitiva de las mareas, de los latidos del corazón, del movimiento convertido en ritual) más que a la mecanización del arte minimalista como modelo de igualdad y de regularidad correlativa.

Otro campo del arte que se relaciona con la práctica y la teoría contemporánea del arte, es un conjunto amplio y sólido de proyectos realizados al aire libre por individuos a menudo llamados artistas de la tierra y el suelo. En tanto que estos títulos describen la obra de artistas que utilizan el exterior como un espacio grande, libre de trabas y no comercial; sin pretender, necesaria o específicamente, crear conexiones con la "naturaleza" (por ejemplo, el Spiral Jetty de Robert Smithson, la manipulación de la tierra de Walter de Maria, los trabajos de tierra y roca de Michael Heizer y los trabajos de Dennis Oppenheim y Robert Morris), también se extienden a artistas que hacen declaraciones, de manera consciente, acerca de la relación de la humanidad con el medio ambiente y, algunas veces, de la naturaleza con lo poético: las construcciones en hielo y las delicadas ramas entrelazadas de Andy Goldsworthy, el cráter alterado de James Turrell para una vista celestial, la proyección de luz y los túneles incluyentes de Nancy Holt, las marcaciones de jardines clásicos de Ian Hamilton Finley y los paisajes esculpidos de Richard Fleischner.[4]

La atención artística de estos artistas y un grupo diverso de otros también se enfoca a obras de escala y propósito dirigidos al paisaje público y urbano (Siah Armajani, Doug Hollis, Maya Lin, Richard Serra, Alice Aycock, Christo), y a un diseño e instalación arquitectónicamente relacionados (desde los edificios de Donald Judd, las casas y paredes de David Ireland, la fragmentación de los elementos arquitectónicos de Gordon Matta-Clark, hasta el mobiliario de Scott Burden). Parte de esta obra revela comentarios de propósito y visión modernos, "sofisticados"; la otra, admite sus orígenes en el ímpetu más primitivo de apilar rocas, de verter agua y de afirmar y sondear las misteriosas e inexplicables iluminaciones de la naturaleza.

La obra de Peter Walker es un híbrido de movimientos y estilos, una investigación de la reserva de cualidades esenciales en el arte de este siglo y su tiempo, que él sondea buscando una revelación. Sus afinidades sintetizan, en su visión y lugar propios, un conjunto de obras que no "encaja" dentro de las categorías o disciplinas establecidas y por lo tanto, nosotros adoptamos la que él mismo continúa usando: diseñador del paisaje. Su obra se relaciona con los minimalistas, no porque él pueda recrear o duplicar un momento crucial en la historia del pensamiento artístico, tener su estilo o crear sus objetos, sino porque algunos aspectos de los vocabularios visuales y mentales del minimalismo, se comparan básicamente con componentes de su propia perspectiva.

Junto con un fuerte compromiso con el valor de lo abstracto, los elementos en serie y lo geométrico como un medio para obtener una revelación en la naturaleza y a través de ella, Peter Walker también ha comprendido el potencial de las características de los movimientos del arte contemporáneo, para satisfacer propósitos pragmáticos y políticos, como contexto para el diseño del paisaje. Los usos de objetualidad independiente del arte minimalista y del trabajo de la tierra, hacen visible el objeto/paisaje, reclaman categoría y espacio y amplían el léxico y esfera de elucidación para su trabajo en el campo. Walker, aceptando siempre la belleza, también abarca el humor, el comentario, la subversión, los juegos de palabras, el diálogo, la colaboración y la poesía. Subyacente a la naturaleza del diseño del paisaje como Walker lo practica, significa la posibilidad de evitar las etiquetas personales, profesionales y artísticas, así como la finalidad de cambiar la forma en que percibimos a y cómo vivimos en nuestro mundo y, en última instancia, de lo que hacemos de nuestro planeta.

[1] Walker, Peter y Melanie Simo. *Invisible Gardens, The Search for Modernism in the American Landscape.* Cambridge: Massachusetts Institute of Technology Press, 1994.

[2] Colpitt, Frances. *Minimal Art: The Critical Perspective.* Seattle: University of Washington Press, 1993.

[3] Tuchman, Maurice, et al. *The Spiritual in Art: Abstract Painting 1890-1985.* Nueva York: Abbeville Press, 1986.

[4] Beardsley, John. *Earthworks and Beyond: Contemporary Art in the Landscape.* Nueva York: Abbeville Press, 1989.

Clasicismo, Modernismo y Minimalismo en el paisaje

Peter Walker

Clasicismo y Modernismo

Los clasicistas definen el Clasicismo literalmente como el estudio de la Grecia clásica y su extensión (resurgimiento), Roma. Cada generación de historiadores del arte, artistas y arquitectos, han definido o redefinido el clasicismo de manera más amplia, para satisfacer el propósito de su época en particular. Cada generación juzga y etiqueta las diferentes subcategorías del clasicismo como buenas o malas (por ejemplo, resurgimiento clásico, neoclásico, etc.), y la pintura, la escultura, la música, la literatura y la arquitectura tienen interpretaciones esotéricas diferentes sobre los significados de estas diferenciaciones.

Sin embargo, parece existir un acuerdo general en cuanto a que ciertas cualidades son inherentes al ideal clásico, tales como la pureza, la claridad, la expresión humana, el origen a partir de la naturaleza y la derivación expresiva a partir de la técnica o el trabajo manual. A partir de estas definiciones más amplias, tal vez sea más fácil ver que cierta cualidad espiritual debe encontrarse en una obra o período para calificarlo como clásico.

Es discutible si el modernismo es, o fue, un movimiento clásico. Evidentemente, los primeros modernistas creían que sí. En su *Vers une Architecture*, de 1923, Le Corbusier compara las primeras grandes obras de ingeniería, los puentes y los transatlánticos con templos griegos. Para mí es difícil no ver a Mies van der Rohe en estos mismos términos, a pesar de sus románticos intereses visuales . Y aún sus posturas reductivistas no eran meras inspiraciones estructurales funcionales. Un sentido ideal de la belleza, parece siempre sobrepasar lo simplemente necesario. Incluso el credo modernista de "menos es más" sólo puede considerarse significativo en su sentido ideal. Tambien Louis Kahn, en su búsqueda de "lo que quiere ser" y su pasión por el movimiento de la luz, parece clásico; pero la sensación de peso en su obra, añade tonos románticos.

El clasicismo en el diseño del paisaje moderno es, tal vez, una línea menos clara. Bien podría decirse que el modernismo del siglo XX, en sí, no se ha realizado en el diseño de jardines tan plenamente como en el de edificios. Sin embargo, yo afirmaría que los jardines se volvieron modernos mucho antes que la arquitectura de fines del siglo XIX y del siglo XX; ya que tanto en los jardines japoneses tradicionales como en los jardines formales del jardinero francés del siglo XVII, Andre Le Nôtre, se manifiestan no sólo el verdadero espíritu del clasicismo, sino también, los principios del modernismo.

Es difícil encontrar ejemplos de jardines clásicos griegos o romanos fuera de las descripciones escritas o dibujadas. Parecen no existir corolarios formales o estilísticos a los órdenes arquitectónicos clásicos. Esto no quiere decir que no existiera un vocabulario aprobado sobre jardines. Los ejes, alamedas, bosques, cuencas, canales, terrazas, senderos, arriates, prados, y cauces, comparten con elementos arquitectónicos, la mayoría de los componentes recurrentes, tanto de los jardines clásicos, como de los posteriores.

También es evidente que el jardín era visto objetivamente como un elemento, aunque, casi siempre, como parte de la arquitectura, determinado por un edificio, una columnata o una pared. Lo que es menos evidente, es la forma como se veía al paisaje común durante la época clásica, separándolo del jardín creado, de la granja o de la parcela agrícola, a la cual, por necesidad, se le daba un cuidado más esmerado que a los jardines en la actualidad.

He aprendido la mayoría de lo que sé acerca de jardines a través de la investigación intuitiva, ya que a diferencia de la erudición, la práctica e incluso la enseñanza, son una empresa no lineal. Como modernista de los últimos de la segunda generación, educado en la década de los años cincuenta, se me negó, junto con una generación de compañeros en las disciplinas del diseño, una visión integral de la historia arquitectónica, debido a que nuestros profesores, incluyendo a Gropius, Giedion y sus seguidores, no nos presentaron la información histórica completa que ellos habían recibido de sus maestros; negándonos la oportunidad de hacer nuestras propias elecciones ideológicas. Por lo tanto, no he tenido la perspectiva histórica que un profesional educado de hace 100 años, razonablemente, pudiera esperar. Por ejemplo, las ideas Le Corbusianas, tales como la expresión de un edificio generada desde el interior, desde su propio plano o diagrama funcional; o sus ideas acerca del objeto arquitectónico en el espacio, no estaban sujetas a discusión, sin importar cuán obviamente limitadas pudieran haber sido. Hasta muy recientemente poco debate o refinamiento teórico se había presentado dentro del modernismo, dejando unidas las ideas legítimas del modernismo con aquellas que, tal vez, debieron ser descartadas. La mayor parte de la crítica, relacionada con el modernismo, se ha presentado en forma de denuncia posterior por parte de los post-modernistas.

La abstracción, había eliminado la mayor parte del contenido expresivo y la narrativa del diseño modernista, además, el pensamiento "internacionalista", generalmente no contemplaba las alusiones a la naturaleza. La finalidad social, democrática o económica, había reemplazado, en gran medida, a la metáfora, aún cuando no estaba claro cómo se lograría un diálogo con los usuarios. Sin este diálogo, o cuando menos un lenguaje aprobado, lo que pudiera significar el "diseño democrático" es una pregunta cuya respuesta todavía se me escapa.

Mi propia obra comenzó como una exploración de dos temas principales. Primero, la extensión de la forma edilicia para crear un medio circundante (léase pedestal) para el objeto preciado, el edificio. El segundo tema era la transición desde este medio al paisaje circundante existente.

Como modernista, a principios de la década de los años setenta, paulatinamente comencé a inquietarme por las tendencias cada vez más pintorescas de mi propia obra, lo cual contrastaba severamente con la obra de arte minimalista de la década de los sesenta que, al mismo tiempo, había estado coleccionando de manera privada. Me parecía que estas obras de arte reflejaban y ampliaban la obra de mis héroes, los primeros arquitectos modernistas, especialmente Mies van der Rohe, Louis Kahn y los arquitectos de estudio de Los Angeles de la década de los años cincuenta.

Me parecía que la obra de la década de los años sesenta de los artistas Frank Stella, Carl Andre, Sol Le Witt, Donald Judd, Dan Flavin, Robert Morris y otros, reafirmaba, y revivía, de forma analítica, la sencillez, la fuerza formal y la claridad que habían sido la mejor parte de mi iniciación educativa al modernismo. Durante estos primeros años, aunque estaba familiarizado con las comparaciones Le Corbusianas entre los templos griegos y los transatlánticos, no relacioné ninguna parte del clasicismo histórico con la empresa del modernismo. Después de todo, la historia había sido definida como el enemigo del modernismo.

En mi interés por desarrollar una teoría de trabajo clásica y moderna de la arquitectura del paisaje, tanto académica como experimental, he identificado dos líneas generales de desarrollo para los paisajes europeos a través de los períodos clásicos. La primera es el desarrollo, principalmente agrícola del campo, que se extiende desde los pueblos y centros urbanos. Hasta principios del siglo XIX éstos fueron el tema de escritos y críticas de figuras tan importantes como John Loudon y Thomas Jefferson. A principios del siglo XIX, el fondo de las pinturas arquitectónicas y de retrato cambió de naturaleza silvestre a agricultura. Durante el siglo XX, la jardinería del paisaje estuvo interesada en asuntos agrícolas en Inglaterra y América del Norte y estos intereses incluían consideraciones estéticas.

La otra línea general de desarrollo fue de extensión arquitectónica. Estos espacios al aire libre, empezando en el siglo XV, fueron diseñados principalmente por arquitectos con la ayuda de jardineros. Generalmente, tomaban la forma de cuartos, terrazas, escalinatas y adornos delimitados arquitectónicamente por piedra y pavimento así como por jardineras utilizadas como piedra. No fue sino hasta que surgió el movimiento paisajista de parques en Francia e Inglaterra en el siglo XVIII que convergieron estas dos líneas de pensamiento, la arquitectónica y la agrícola. Sin embargo, en ese momento, los aspectos pintorescos agobiaban el desarrollo formal o geométrico de los trescientos años anteriores. Para el ojo no educado, estos no representaban arte, sino a la naturaleza misma.

Este aspecto pictórico eclipsó los logros de los grandes jardines del châteaux y particularmente aquellos de Andre Le Nôtre. Ha existido la idea de que los jardines ingleses eran más una expresión del modernismo debido a que representan la "naturaleza". Frederick Law Olmsted hizo mucho a partir de esta idea y la consideraba terapéutica para los males del urbanismo industrial. Ian McHarg también ha adoptado este concepto en su ataque a los jardines franceses y renacentistas. Sin embargo, los jardines franceses podrían representar una línea de investigación más clásica ya que éstos representan claramente la forma más elevada de la progresión agrícola proveniente de los siglos XII y XIII. La reestructuración del paisaje agrícola francés (y más tarde el inglés) se logró debido a las técnicas administrativas de la iglesia, en su esfuerzo por financiar y construir las catedrales a través de la labranza del campo. En las obras de Le Nôtre, se pueden ver claramente, las hileras de arbustos, las áreas boscosas y los estanques de tierras bajas drenadas, así como las geometrías directas del ambiente rural francés. Indudablemente, éstas son expresiones clásicas de la naturaleza, tanto como los jardines pictóricos más románticos.

En Asia, el jardín se consideraba como una forma artística separada de la arquitectura o la agricultura, con un valor y autonomía paralelos a las artes de la pintura, la escultura, la música y la poesía. Se concibió, tanto un lenguaje de forma, como una gran gama de escalas de expresión. El cultivo y refinamiento de estos jardines son, en muchas formas, análogos a aquellos de la arquitectura clásica occidental.

El modernismo aún tiene que desarollar un conjunto articulado de teoría del paisaje, aunque se pueden ver, en las pocas obras maestras, exploraciones de múltiples propuestas formales tomadas de los diversos estilos artísticos o combinaciones de ellos, tales como el constructivismo o el surrealismo.

Con la excepción del breve movimiento francés del jardín durante la década de los años veinte, ni el De Stijl, la Bauhaus ni el CIAM han considerado el diseño del paisaje, de una forma esencial o principal. Ellos visualizaron, generalmente el espacio abierto y la naturaleza, como espacio "vacío" y cuantitativo en el cual instalar construcciones, más que como actos de diseño objetivos y cualitativos. Se consideraba que este espacio abierto funcionaba de manera similar a la caja blanca de la galería o museo modernos, como un ambiente neutro. Hasta ahora, la mayoría de los arquitectos tienen una idea más bien romántica del paisaje como de naturaleza silvestre o de un ambiente "suave". Los primeros arquitectos modernistas fueron iniciados en el diseño del paisaje, primero en Inglaterra y de forma más enfática en los Estados Unidos a fines de la década de los años treinta cuando los líderes de estos movimientos huyeron de Alemania y otras partes de Europa y empezaron a enseñar en universidades norteamericanas.

Mi trabajo durante los últimos 20 años ha sido un intento de entrelazar los hilos del clasicismo, del formalismo de los jardines europeos y asiáticos y los del modernismo, incluyendo al modernista reciente y al minimalista de mediados de siglo, como yo los entiendo. El resultado es lo que considero minimalismo en el paisaje.

El Minimalismo en el paisaje

El minimalismo en el paisaje, a diferencia de lo específico de su argumento artístico mundial relacionado con un cierto grupo de artistas, en un cierto momento durante la década de los años sesenta, me parece a mí que representa un renacimiento de los intereses analíticos de los primeros modernistas, los cuales se comparan, en muchos aspectos, con el espíritu del clasicismo. Es la reinvención formal y la búsqueda de la pureza primaria y el sentido humano lo que significa su fuerza espiritual: así, un interés por el misterio y el contenido no referencial, están ligados a la búsqueda del pensamiento clásico.

Así como el término e idea del clasicismo, el minimalismo ha entrado a nuestra presurada sociedad y ha sido aún más definido y redefinido por diversas disciplinas artísticas y culturales. En este contexto más amplio, el minimalismo continúa implicando una propuesta que rechaza cualquier intento de superar las fuerzas de la naturaleza, intelectual, técnica o industrialmente. Este propone un orden conceptual y la realidad de cambiar los sistemas naturales por medio de la geometría, la narrativa, el ritmo, el gesto y otros recursos que puedan impregnar el espacio con un sentido de paraje único que vive en la memoria.

A pesar del alcance más amplio del uso que hago del término minimalismo, la referencia a un artista, quintaesencia del minimalismo, es iluminante. Donald Judd insistió en que el minimalismo es, ante todo, una expresión del objetivo, un enfoque del objeto mismo, más que su contexto circundante o su interpretación. El minimalismo no es representativo ni referencial, aún cuando algunos espectadores, inevitablemente, harán sus propias proyecciones históricas o icónicas. En correlación con esto, aunque el paisaje minimalista existe en el contexto más extenso del medio ambiente, y aunque éste puede emplear estrategias de interrupción o interacción y se puede ver más allá de los "objetos" diseñados hacia el paisaje más amplio, el foco se encuentra aún en el propio paisaje diseñado, en su propia energía y espacio. La escala, tanto en el contexto como la experimentada internamente, continúa siendo primordialmente importante. Así como en el arte minimalista, el paisaje minimalista no es, necesaria ni esencialmente, reductivista; aunque estas obras, a menudo, tienen componentes mínimos y una franqueza que implica sencillez.

Con estos parámetros, el minimalismo en la arquitectura del paisaje abre una línea de cuestionamiento que puede iluminarnos y guiarnos a través de algunas de las transiciones difíciles de nuestro tiempo: la simplificación o pérdida artesanal, las transiciones de los materiales naturales tradicionales a los sintéticos y las extensiones de la escala humana a la gran escala, tanto en espacio como en tiempo, de nuestra vida moderna mecanizada. Así mismo, el minimalismo en este contexto sugiere una propuesta artísticamente exitosa para tratar con dos de los problemas ambientales más críticos que enfrentamos actualmente: los desechos crecientes y la disminución de los recursos.

Una investigación acerca del minimalismo en el paisaje parece estar especialmente a tiempo en la actualidad. Las tendencias recientes en arquitectura del paisaje, arquitectura y diseño urbano durante lo que se ha llamado nuestra era post-moderna, han cuestionado la legitimidad del diseño modernista y algunas favorecen un regreso al clasicismo. Mucho del trabajo y pensamiento reciente en esta área se ha enfocado, por una parte, a los aspectos formales y decorativos y, por la otra, a los aspectos sociológicos y funcionales. El minimalismo, una de las manifestaciones de fines del alto modernismo en las artes visuales, tiene en sí, por supuesto, muchas fuertes obligatorias con el clasicismo. Más que enfocarse a aspectos funcionales y de diseño como mutuamente exclusivos, el minimalismo guía al examen de lo abstracto y lo esencial, cualidades tanto del diseño clasicista como del modernista.

Es interesante recordar que cuando el joven Le Corbusier viajó a través de las tierras del Medio Oriente y del Mediterráneo, antes de la Primera Guerra Mundial en 1911, fue atraído hacia las mezquitas turcas, los monasterios bizantinos y las casas búlgaras, debido a ciertas cualidades, particularmente, el silencio, la luz y la forma simple y austera. Sin embargo, en la Acrópolis de Atenas, estaba abrumado y admirado por el Partenón "el maestro innegable", el cual, más tarde, interpretó como una destilación de la forma, un producto insuperable de estandarización. El dedujo que se había llegado a un momento en el que no podía quitarse nada más. Fue un momento de perfección, un definir de lo clásico. Sucede que yo tuve una respuesta similar ante un jardín en particular, de Le Nôtre, cuando lo visité en 1970. Chantilly, un gran jardín de piedra, agua, espacio y luz, también representa un ejemplo soberbio de la forma reducida a su perfección esencial. Chantilly me pareció entonces y aún me sigue pareciendo que comparte, en su esencia, un entendimiento e intención que son, tanto clásico como minimalistas.

Estos pensamientos son, de alguna manera, un informe del progreso de mi viaje personal como un arquitecto del paisaje que llegó a la mayoría de edad durante la cumbre del modernismo en el diseño ambiental norteamericano. Estos están alimentados por los jardines, paisajes, diseños, artistas y discernimientos que han ayudado a moldear mis percepciones y a trazar mi particular curso de investigación hasta este momento. Ofrecen una propuesta personal para la creación de entornos que parecen ser especialmente necesarios en estos momentos de la historia de la humanidad: entornos que son serenos y ordenados y aún así, expresivos y significativos. Más que nunca, necesitamos incorporar, en nuestro entorno construido, lugares de reunión, de congregación, de eficiencia, junto con espacios para el descubrimiento, reposo e intimidad en nuestro jardín, cada vez más confuso, espiritualmente empobrecido, atestado y poco conservado: la Tierra.

El arte no es un jardín

Mi transición de persona que aprecia el arte a mi preocupación de integrar ideas sobre el arte en mi obra del paisaje, fue gradual. Al principio, yo era un coleccionista, frecuentaba galerías y leía, vorazmente, libros, revistas de arte y catálogos, especialmente acerca de los minimalistas. Pensaba que no había un propósito profesional ni un pensamiento entrecruzado en mi interés, solamente la curiosidad sobre la belleza y el significado del arte, así como la energía visual e intelectual que éste genera.

Después de varios años, recuerdo haber notado lo que yo imaginaba como ideas de paisaje en las primeras pinturas rayadas de Frank Stella: cómo el diseño interno de las figuras era capaz de definir la forma de una pintura bidimensional, obviando el marco y eliminando la posibilidad de ser interpretado como una imagen abstracta. Esto era como un jardín sin paredes, capaz de existir en un contexto espacial y también de ser un objeto aparte.

Entonces, las piezas metálicas para piso de Carl Andre, empezaron a parecerme poderosas metáforas de jardines: todo en un solo plano, sobre el piso y casi sin tercera dimensión, y aún así, controlando completamente el carácter y naturaleza del espacio "vacío" superior. Estos me recordaba los tapetes persas del desierto beduino: jardines móviles, íntimos e ideales. Una obra de Andre de 1973, "*144 Blocks and Stones*" fue especialmente dinámico por medio de esta interpretación. Para su instalación, se vaciaron todas las paredes (léase arquitectura) de la galería y el piso (léase paisaje) se convirtió en un misterioso tótem o juego. Los materiales eran modestos, incluso mundanos, pero el resultado fue intensamente imponente y experimenté una fuerte conexión entre los misteriosos espíritus del arte y los jardines.

Sin embargo, otra obra de Andre de 1977, "*Secant*", se colocó en una pradera común. La pradera era hermosa de manera natural, pero difícilmente diferente de miles como ella en la región. Por medio de la colocación que hizo Andre, profundamente simple, de una serie de maderos cortados, la pradera se transformó en un lugar que generaba y exigía una memoria consciente e inconsciente.

De manera semejante, la "*Running Fence*", 1972-1976 de Christo, fue construida en un paisaje genérico de colinas que se extendían hacia el oeste del Océano Pacífico en los condados de Marin y Sonoma en California y le dio vida al paisaje logrando una condición de intensa celebración. Yo había crecido y vivido la mayor parte de mi vida en esas mismas colinas costeras y pensé que las conocía mejor que la mayoría y más que a cualquier otro paisaje de mi experiencia. Sin embargo, nunca las había visto realmente en esta forma o nunca antes me había sentido, tan intensamente, como parte de ellas. Era asombroso que una fila de lienzos sedosos pudieran lograr tal modificación. Aún así, en ese momento no pude ver relación directa alguna entre mi respuesta y emoción como espectador con algo que hubiera pensado o creado como arquitecto del paisaje.

Con el tiempo, más obras de arte fortalecieron y expandieron mi creciente sentido del potencial para la integración del arte y el paisaje y, finalmente, descubrí que no estaba satisfecho con sólo coleccionar obras de arte. Después de hacer un recorrido por jardines franceses, un verano a fines de la década de los años setenta, se concretó la cohesión entre los magníficos jardines históricos formales, el arte del minimalismo y mi propia visión de la arquitectura del paisaje y empecé a tratar de crear jardines en forma diferente. Los primeros esfuerzos fueron meramente tentativos. Se hizo patente que la simple transferencia de una idea artística inspirada por la obra en una galería o en un lugar específico, no sería, por sí misma, una estrategia de éxito, ni siquiera un nuevo rumbo en la arquitectura del paisaje, dadas las otras dimensiones de la naturaleza que debían incluirse.

Aún cuando el concepto de objetualidad era útil, por ejemplo, la idea de expresar un significado no podía aislarse de otras consideraciones apremiantes. Los objetos y sistemas formales se perciben en el paisaje, en intenso contraste con el entorno más amplio, que incluye no sólo los pormenores de un lugar y sus alrededores, sino, de manera más completa, los ritmos orgánicos del movimiento diario del sol y la luna, los cambios de la luz estacional, así como de clima y, especialmente, los actos extremos de la naturaleza y las características más fortuitas del nacimiento, el crecimiento y la decadencia. Esta compleja interacción entre la naturaleza y aún el más simple de los objetos instalado o colocado, aumenta y combina la expectativa y la tolerancia necesarias para concebir la obra sobre la tierra, haciendo del tiempo un factor tan grande como el lugar.

Esta comprensión, aunque nueva para mí en ese momento en la magnitud de su claridad, es, no obstante, realmente obvia. Sin embargo, en el campo del diseño del paisaje contemporáneo, el elemento del tiempo y la realidad de lo que no se puede predecir, con frecuencia no se consideran como prioridad debido a tres razones eminentemente cartesianas. La primera es que todavía predomina una tendencia científica/tecnológica de querer disectar, vencer y controlar, en lugar de celebrar el misterio de la naturaleza. Después, persiste una incapacidad o renuencia para tratar con la complejidad y el cambio naturales en nuestro deseo de ofrecer un servicio "experto". (Tal vez lo fácil de predecir ocupa un lugar demasiado elevado en nuestro sistema de valores). Y en tercer lugar, existe un énfasis exagerado en el programa detallado y específico, derivado de una aceptación cuestionable del pensamiento arquitectónico modernista.

Si "la forma precede a la función", entonces, analizar la función para hacer que la forma le siga, se convierte en la prioridad. Por lo tanto, la forma expresa o revela meramente la función sobre cualquier otro ideal superior como una medida de satisfacción de los objetivos del diseño. La propuesta artística más intuitiva de diseñar en y con la naturaleza y, en principio, el plan más generalizado y universal revelan las propiedades y prospectos maravillosos de la interacción entre un acto humano físico y el siempre cambiante mundo del espacio abierto.

Entonces, el verdadero problema con mi consideración real y conceptual de la arquitectura del paisaje, fue que existía una abundancia de ideas centrales disponibles, pero los parámetros para elegir algunas que resonasen en una forma útil, significativa, hermosa e incluso misteriosa o espiritual, estaban aún, indeterminados.

La combinación poco probable del pensamiento y arte de los minimalistas y las condiciones del espacio abierto natural, no conscientizada por los diseñadores contemporáneos del paisaje, abrió un camino de investigación y experimentación fascinante y desafiante. Con esta forma de ver el problema, resulta una revelación el tratar con todos los aspectos del ámbito público (incluyendo tierras abandonadas, calles, estacionamientos, azoteas, así como las búsquedas más tradicionales de jardines, parques y plazas). Esto ofrece una base para reexaminar nuestras ciudades y suburbios, antiguos y nuevos.

Visibilidad

Yo creo que para que un objeto sea visible, debe verse en y por sí mismo, por lo menos de manera parcial. Si está subordinado en gran medida al contexto o si se confunde con alguna forma existente del entorno, se priva a la obra de su capacidad de ser expresiva, de contener significado o narrativa o de grabarse en la memoria. Incluso la alta decoración no puede atraer una atención consciente si no puede lograr objetualidad junto a las otras presencias artísticas existentes.

La sociedad moderna es comercial y está fragmentada. El paisaje se ve como abierto y vacío y mucho del espacio urbano moderno se deja de lado, al margen, abandonado. Los símbolos de conmemoración han decaído. Las imágenes naturales, históricas y remotas están reemplazando rápidamente a la verdadera experiencia al aire libre. Entonces, ¿cuáles son las posibles estrategias para la visibilidad, dadas estas condiciones?

La fragmentación, tanto física como experimental, tiende a dañar nuestro sentido del orden natural. Los arroyos se interrumpen y entuban; las colinas y montañas se cortan, se eliminan o se cubren visualmente de cicatrices. Las vías peatonales estan hechas en forma discontinua. Las construcciones y la contaminación química, obstruyen las líneas visuales naturales del lugar hacia las principales formas definitorias de la tierra, incluyendo el mar e incluso el cielo. Los caminos, carreteras y edificaciones hechos por el hombre, y en algunos casos, también los paisajes creados por éste, han debilitado visualmente las unidades naturales distintivas del paisaje, tales como la Cuenca de Los Angeles, la isla de Manhattan, el Río Charles en Boston así como miríadas de otros ejemplos.

Implícito en estas mutaciones, existe un sentido disminuido del orden, la tranquilidad, las dimensiones visuales y la pérdida de estabilidad que los humanos premodernos encontraron en las montañas, las praderas, los lagos, los ríos y mares, los desarrollos agrícolas, los pueblos y los pequeños asentamientos urbanos. En todas estas situaciones, los ordenamientos espaciales, aludían a una vasta naturaleza que duplicaba una relación con la tierra como un todo.

Si el simple orden, por sí solo, contrasta intensamente con la fragmentación, la discontinuidad y la marginación, entonces, los valores de la reducción y del enfoque, ofrecen un camino para nuestra cultura. Los recursos de orden, comunes a mucho del arte minimalista y a los jardines formales tradicionales, incluyen los arreglos en serie y la repetición, la geometría (especialmente las cuadrículas lineales y de punto), las extensiones perceptibles de dimensiones, los gestos lineales y la explotación visual de los centros y de los contornos, incluyendo simetría bilateral y la asimétrica. La exploración de textura y diseño, de escala y contraste de color, así como de lo sintético contra lo natural, lo vivo contra lo inerte, en este contexto, también son caminos hacia el orden. A esta lista cabe añadir la conmemoración, la narrativa y el símbolo. Finalmente, con la necesidad de volver el análisis hacia las propiedades visuales esenciales, el objetivo es lograr misterio más que ironía.

El paisaje como arte

El espacio al aire libre es igualmente importante, o tal vez más crucial, que el espacio interior para la vida social moderna, cívica y cultural. El paisaje diseñado puede tener tanta capacidad de expresión conmemorativa o de misterio como cualquier fachada u otra forma o dimensión arquitectónica. El espacio público al aire libre creado únicamente para funcionar, lleno de caminos con un fin determinado pero desnudos artísticamente, espacios para estacionamiento y servicio, por ejemplo, es el que lleva el mensaje de fealdad indiferente, empañando con esto las esperanzas del modernismo al grado de sentir que el modernismo, de hecho, ha fallado. Gran parte de este fracaso yace en la planificación del emplazamiento y de las áreas al aire libre, el ámbito público de ciudades y pueblos.

Uno de los temas de la arquitectura clásica es la alusión a regresar a la naturaleza y la búsqueda del ideal clásico a través de generaciones de invención, reinterpretación, expresión y entrelazamiento de estos temas con aquellos de una cultura próspera y siempre creciente. Entonces, ¿cómo puede uno imaginar un paralelo dentro de una forma de arte que es en sí, en gran parte, naturaleza? Creo que la respuesta pudiera yacer en la capacidad de ver la naturaleza en dos formas, tanto indómita como dócil.

La naturaleza indómita y el paisaje abierto nunca se encuentran en un estado de estabilidad o permanencia como es el estado que implica la arquitectura clásica. Por lo tanto, la arquitectura es una analogía pobre para el paisaje. Aunque frecuentemente la música describía el paisaje, es demasiado efímera y aún cuando se puede describir el paisaje con la música (por ejemplo, la obra de John Cage), no es físicamente habitable como lo es el espacio abierto. Este, es un medio muy complejo en el cual influir, sujeto como está, a los múltiples cambios constantes de los ciclos diarios, estacionales y de maduración, así mismo complicado por el sonido, el olor, la temperatura y la precipitación. De todas las artes, se compara de manera más cercana con la complejidad de la vida humana.

Una naturaleza en constante cambio, define una forma de arte diferente, única en sí misma y separada de las otras. Los criterios existentes todavía se encuentran en estado de creación, aún abiertos al desarrollo, la expansión, el diálogo, la posibilidad, la dirección y la esperanza.

Existen muchas preguntas a considerar: ¿Es demasiado extravagante? ¿Se puede controlar suficientemente el paisaje moderno (natural o urbano) como para ser contexto y contenido de una forma artística? ¿Puede una concepción del paisaje proporcionar suficiente control dentro de la complejidad de la existencia moderna? En otras palabras, ¿pueden los medios con los que contamos lograr los fines que buscamos? Yo siento que pueden, y que las guías hacia ese éxito se encuentran en las obras innovadoras de Luis Barragán, Isamu Noguchi, Roberto Burle Marx, Dan Kiley, Lawrence Halprin y los otros grandes diseñadores del paisaje de nuestro tiempo. Para mí, el minimalismo es una línea de cuestionamiento que nos dirige a la infinidad de soluciones que nuestra cultura espera.

Dialog mit dem Lande: die Kunst Peter Walkers

Leah Levy

Unsere zeitgenössische Kategorisierung der geschaffenen Landschaft wird konsistent und bewußt in direktem Abhängigkeitsverhältnis mit der Architektur gesehen. So wird der Architekt der Landschaft typischerweise auf die Planung des Raumes zwischen den architektonischen Strukturen verwiesen, welche ihrerseits die sichtbarsten Monumente in der Landschaft ausmachen. In den heutigen Universitäten trifft man auf die Fächer der Architektur und der Landschaftsarchitektur in derselben Abteilung, da die Landschaftsarchitektur sich von ihrer früheren Assoziation mit Landwirtschaft und Gartenbau entfernt hat. Der herkömmliche Wortschatz zur Beschreibung der entworfenen Landschaft und des Gartens ist der Architektur und der Landwirtschaft entlehnt.

Um die Arbeit Peter Walkers genauer zu betrachten, reichen die konventionellen Wertmaßstäbe für Landschaftsarchitektur und Gärten nicht aus. Walkers ausgereifte Arbeiten spezialisieren sich auf die Sichtbarkeit der Landschaft durch Design. SeinAnspruch schließt dieses Gebiet als unabhängige Einheit mit Rang und Status mit ein, was den bildenden Künsten und der Architektur vergleichbar ist. Die vorhandene kritische Literatur bezüglich der kreierten Landschaft ist aber im Vergleich zur Literatur über andere Künste sehr mager.

Walkers Stilmerkmale kann man auf verschiedenartige und doch logisch verbundene Ursprünge zurückführen. Archetypische und primitive Spuren in der Landschaft, wie zum Beispiel die Nazca Linien in Peru und Stonehenge in England, stellen ein menschliches Grundbedürfnis die Umgebung zu markieren dar. Das ist ein menschliches Bedürfnis, sich mit dem größeren Umfeld auseinanderzusetzen, ein Bewußtsein von–und einer Frage nach–derVerbindung mit weltlichen und himmlischen Geheimnissen zu signalisieren und auf die Gewalt der überirdischen Kräfte anzuspielen, liegt vielen Werken Walkers zugrunde. In vielen Fällen konzentriert sich die Arbeit auf die rätselhaften Qualitäten der Natur, die das Geräusch des Wassers verkörpert, die Aufstapelung und das Gewicht des Steines, die rauschende Veränderung des Windes, die Blöcke und Muster sich ändernder Farben, der magisch schimmernde Nebel und das täuschende Licht.

In ähnlichem Zusammenhang dient die klassische Ordnung der französischen Gärten des 17. Jahrhunderts, besonders der von André Le Notre, als starker Vorläufer zu individuellen Elementen in Walkers Stil. Seine intuitive und intellektuelle Vorliebe für Muster, Rhythmus und Ordnung und für eine Art kartesischer Synthese, ist in seiner Arbeit immer wieder auffällig. Ebenso unübersehbar ist der Einfluß der Zengärten in Walkers Arbeit. In den klaren Komponenten und der vereinenden Ganzheit vieler seiner Entwürfe wird ein zugrundeliegender, philosophischer Destillierprozess vom Komplexen zum Einfachen, sichtbar.

Walkers Arbeit bezieht sich auch auf die Entwicklung der modernen Landschaftsarchitektur. Er ist unermüdlich damit befaßt, die Geschichte der Landschaftsarchitektur seines Jahrhunderts zu beleuchten und hervorzuheben.[1] Ganz besonders waren die Gärten der Mitte des 20. Jahrhunderts von Thomas Church und Isamu Noguchi während seiner Studienjahre Quellen seiner Inspiration. Um sich jedoch effektiv mit dem Erfolg und der Bedeutung Walkers Landschaften, mit ihrem Rang in zeitgenössischer Kultur und dem anhaltenden Dialog seiner gedanklichen und praktischen Beschäftigung mit der Kunst, auseinanderzusetzen, ist eine Analyse der wesentlichen, künstlerischen Entwicklungen des 20. Jahrhunderts der effektivste Weg diese Arbeit im gegenwärtigen kulturellen Zusammenhang zu sehen.

Die frühen Jahrzehnte dieses Jahrhunderts waren angefüllt mit Neuheiten in Kunst, Wissenschaft und Kultur, die durch das ganze Jahrhundert hindurch maßgebend wirkten. Einer neuen Wahrnehmung lag der Pioniergedanke der puren Abstraktion in der visuellen Kunst zugrunde; das heißt Kunst, die sich weder auf einen wahren oder physischen Gegenstand bezog, noch ihm imitierte, die aber in ihrer unabhängigen und abstrakten Form als komplettes Mittel des Ausdrucks und der Erforschung diente. Die Geometrie vieler dieser Originalwerke, besonders der frühen russischen Konstruktivisten, hatte das Anliegen universale Geheimnisse, die die Menschheit zeitlebens zu ergründen suchte und darzustellen: Wege des Abtastens und Verstehens der Phänomene, die man erleben, aber denen man nicht mit einem traditionellen Realitätsverständnis beikommen kann.

Befreit also von der Geschichte und wörtlichen Assoziationen, konnte die zwei- und dreidimensionale Kunst, wie zum Beispiel die Musik, als unabhängiges Erlebnis verstanden werden ohne die Absicht, ein spezifisches, erkennbares Resultat zu erzielen und mit völlig neuer Freiheit für den Künstler und Betrachter ihre Reaktionen auf einer höheren als der bewußten Ebene stattfinden zu lassen.

Ein anderes Beispiel des erfinderischen Geistes des frühen 20. Jahrhunderts ist das Werk des französischen Künstlers Marcel Duchamp, der das Objekt (tatsächlich oder abstrakt) in seiner

Schönheit und Bedeutung ablehnte und das Gebiet des Künstlers in eine undefinierbare Kunst des Gemütes erweiterte. Duchamp forderte für den Künstler das Recht zu bestimmen, was als Kunst gelten soll und erweiterte damit die Arena des künstlerischen Experimentierens. Indem er die Parameter künstlerischer Kategorien verwischte und den Kunststatus auf nicht-kunstähnliche Objekte und Ideen übertrug, schaffte Duchamp Möglichkeiten für Künstler, die weit über die Tradition von Malerei und Bildhauerei hinausreichten und in der heutigen Kunstwelt weiterhin richtungsweisend sind.

Neben sozialen, politischen und kulturellen Einflüßen fand der Minimalismus seine geschichtlichen Wurzeln im Durchbruch der Abstraktionisten als auch in den führenden Theorien Duchamps. Seit seinem Höhepunkt in den 60er Jahren ist Minimalismus, möglicherweise die erste rein amerikanische Kunstform, zum losen, alles umschreibenden Begriff geworden, den die Kultur aufgegriffen hat, um Stile zu bezeichnen, die nicht figürlich, nicht Stellung nehmend, die geometrisch oder einfach spärlich in der Verwendung von Materialien sind.

Der Begriff der minimalen Kunst ist jedoch ca. 1963-68 geprägt worden, um einen ganz bestimmten Zeitraum zu identifizieren und eine kleine Gruppierung von Künstlern, die vornehmlich in New York City arbeiteten, nämlich Donald Judd, Dan Flavin, Sol Lewitt, Robert Morris und Carl Andre. Die Arbeit dieser Künstler stellt eine philosophische Basis dar, die jegliche Versuche traditioneller Kategorisierung vermeidet. Das Hauptanliegen der Künstler sei es, raumbeherrschende Objekte zu schaffen, die in physischem Zusammenhang mit dem Betrachter, der selbst Raum einnimmt, wahrgenommen werden würden[2], eine "nicht wiedergebbare Kommunikation".[3] Die Materialien als Objekte im Raum waren Thema und Inhalt der minimalistischen Kunst und erforderten vom Betrachter direkt wahrgenommen und körperlich erfahren zu werden. Mit dem Ziel im Auge, einen Weg zur Schaffung primärer Objekte mit primärer Wirkung, fanden die minimalistischen Künstler Methoden, ihre Resultate zu reduzieren.

Da der Inhalt dieser Kunst die Beziehung des Objekts und seiner Umgebung zum Betrachter war, wurden die Arbeiten häufig als formalistisch bezeichnet: sie konnten beschrieben werden (mit Begriffen wie etwa Größe, Form, Farbe), jedoch ohne das Erlebnis des Umschreitens, Durchwanderns und Hineinkletterns konnten sie nicht gedeutet werden. Eingeschlossen in eine lange Reihe formaler Züge dieser Arbeiten, waren die Verwendung einfacher und geometrischer Formen, die Wiederholung und systematische Anordnung von Objekten, der Gebrauch moderner Materialien und industrieller Produkte, die Dreidimensionalität (obwohl man vom skulpturellen ablenken wollte), die Grundfarben und die Plazierung der Strukturen direkt am Boden, an der Wand lehnend und in unmittelbarem Bezug zum Raum, ohne Podest oder Rahmen.

Ein weiterer wesentlicher Charakterzug der Werke der minimalistischen Kunstepoche ist der Rahmen, in dem sie installiert und ausgestellt wurden, ob im weißen Würfel der Gallerie oder draußen in der Natur. Da sie die physische und phänomenologische Beziehung zwischen den Objekten, dem menschlichen Körper und dem Raum, der sie enthielt hervorheben sollten, wurde oft großen Wert auf die Kalkulation der Größenverhältnisse aller Elemente gelegt.

Während sich Peter Walkers Arbeit an die Sensibilität der formalen Ästhetik des 20. Jahrhunderts anlehnt, die sich in der Kultur und Arbeit der minimalistischen Künstler manifestiert, scheint sie ebenso starke Verbindung mit anderen Künstlergruppen des 20. Jahrhunderts zu haben. Diese Künstler, deren Arbeiten eine systematisch formalistische Abstraktion, verstanden als Teil des Minimalismus, eigen ist, geben der Kunst einen ganz anderen philosophischen Hintergrund. Maler und Bildhauer wie Ad Reinhardt, Agnes Martin, Robert Ryman, Robert Mangold, Ellsworth Kelly, Porfirio DiDonna, Yves Klein, Jasper Johns, Robert Irwin haben ihre Abstraktionen auf unterschwelligeres Suchen und Deuten ausgerichtet. In einigen dieser Werke beziehen sich Rhythmen und wiederholte Muster eher auf organische Systeme und die Kadenz der Dichtung (die sich wiederholende Rhytmik von Ebbe und Flut, des Herzschlags, der ritualisierten Bewegung), als auf die Mechanisierung der minimalistischen Kunst als Modum für Verworrenheit und relative Regelmäßigkeit.

Ein weiteres Kunstgebiet, das auf sich zeitgenössischer Kunsttheorie und -praxis beruht, ist ein breitgefächertes Spektrum verschiedenster Projekte, von Individuen konzipiert, die häufig als Land- und Erdkünstler bezeichnet werden. Dieser Überbegriff beschreibt die Arbeit von Künstlern, die die Natur als großen, ungestörten, unkommerziellen Raum benutzen, ohne unbedingt einen Bezug zur "Natur" herstellen zu wollen (Robert Smithons Spiral Jetty, die Landmanipulationen von Walter de Maria, Michael Heizers Erd- und Felsarbeiten und Arbeiten von Dennis Oppenheim und Robert Morris zum Beispiel). Er bezieht sich allerdings im weiten Rahmen auch auf Künstler, die bewußt eine Aussage über die Beziehung der Menschheit zu ihrem Umfeld machen, und manchmal über die der Natur zur Dichtung: Andy Goldworthys Eiskonstruktionen und delikate Zweiggewebe, James Turrells veränderter Krater zur himmlischen Betrachtung, die Licht projizierenden und enthaltenden Tunnel von Nancy Holt, Ian Hamilton Finleys klassische

Gartenkonzepte und die Landschaften von Richard Fleischner.[4]

Der künstlerische Brennpunkt dieser einer sehr heterogenen Gruppe anderer Künstler beinhaltet auch eine Skala, die die öffentliche und städtische Landschaft anspricht, (Siah Armajani, Doug Hollis, Maya Lin, Richard Serra, Alice Aycock, Christo), als auch architekturbezogene Installationsdesigns (von Donald Judds Gebäuden, David Irelands Häusern und Wänden, Gordon Matta-Clarks Fragmentierung von Architekturelementen zu den Möbeln von Scott Burden). Einige dieser Werke geben Kommentar zur aufgeklärten modernen Vision und Intention; andere erkennen ihren Ursprung an im primitivsten Impuls, Felsen aufzutürmen, Wasser zu gießen und die mysteriösen und unerklärbaren Beleuchtungen der Natur zu erforschen und zur Geltung zu bringen.

Peter Walkers Arbeit beruht auf einer Mischung von Bewegungen und Stilarten, einer Untersuchung des Reservoirs wesentlicher Qualitäten in der Kunst des Jahrhunderts und seiner Zeit, die er auf der Suche nach Offenbarung anzapft. Seine Neigungen verschmelzen in seiner eigenen, einzigartigen Vision, einem Arbeitsvolumen, das nicht in etablierte Kategorien paßt, und so adoptieren wir ein Landschaftsdesign, das er selbst ständig anwendet. Seine Arbeit bezieht sich nicht auf die Minimalisten, weil sie einen wichtigen, geschichtlichen Moment künstlerischen Denkens erneuert oder kopiert, sein Aussehen hat oder seine Objekte schafft, sondern weil Aspekte des visuellen und geistigen Vokabulars des Minimalismus den Komponenten Walkers eigener Perspektive wesensmäßig ähnlich sind.

Nebendem Peter Walker sich auf den Wert des Abstrakten, des Serienmäßigen und des Geometrischen festlegte, als einen Weg, Offenbarungen in und durch Natur zu erreichen, hat er auch das Potential der zeitgenössischen Kunstbewegungen aufgegriffen, welchem pragmatische und politische Ziele als Kontext für Landschaftsdesign zugrunde liegt. Minimalistische Kunst und Erdarbeitsapplikationen unabhängiger Objekte machen das Objekt bzw. die Landschaft sichtbar, verlangen nach Status und Raum und erweitern das Lexikon und die Sphäre der Aufklärung für seine Arbeit mit der Landschaft. Indem Walker immer der Schönheit den Vorrang gibt, macht Walker sich auch Humor, Kommentar, Umsturz, Wortspiel, Dialog, Kollaboration und Dichtung zu eigen. Die Eigenart von Walkers Landschaftsdesignpraxis ist es, einen persönlichen, beruflichen und künstlerischen Stempel zu vermeiden, als auch das Ziel, unsere Wahrnehmung von und unsere Lebensweise in der Welt zu verändern und schließlich die Fragestellung, was wir aus unserem Planeten machen.

[1] Walker, Peter und Melanie Simo. *Invisible Gardens, The Search for Modernism in the American Landscape*. Cambridge: Massachusetts Institute of Technology Press, 1994.

[2] Colpitt, Frances. *Minimal Art: The Critical Perspective*. Seattle: University of Washington Press, 1993.

[3] Tuchman, Maurice, et al. *The Spiritual in Art: Abstract Painting 1890-1985*. New York: Abbeville Press, 1986.

[4] Beardsley, John. *Earthworks and Beyond: Contemporary Art in the Landscape*. New York: Abbeville Press, 1989.

Klassizismus, Modernismus und Minimalismus in der Landschaft

von Peter Walker

Klassizismus und Modernismus

Von Altphilologen wird das Studium des klassischen Griechenlands und seiner Ausbreitung und Erneuerung durch Rom als Klassizismus definiert. Jede Epoche von Kunsthistorikern, Künstlern und Architekten hat den Klassizismus entweder erweitert oder neu definiert, um dem Bedarf der Zeit gerecht zu werden. Verschiedene Kategorien des Begriffs werden aber in den jeweiligen Epochen benannt und als positiv oder negativ beurteilt (z.B., klassische Erneuerung, Neoklassizismus u.s.w.). Sogar die Malerei, die Bildhauerei, die Musik, die Literatur und die Architektur haben unterschiedliche, esoterische Auffassungen von der Bedeutung dieser Beurteilungen entwickelt.

Es scheint allgemeine Übereinstimmung darüber zu herrschen, daß dem klassischen Ideal gewisse Merkmale eigen sind: Reinheit, Klarheit, Ausdruck von Menschlichkeit, Ursprünglichkeit in der Natur und eine eindeutige Beziehung zur Handwerkskunst oder Technik. Solche weitgefassten Definitionen ermöglichen wohl die Einsicht, daß ein Werk oder eine Epoche gewisse geistige Eigenschaften besitzen muß, um als klassisch eingestuft zu werden.

Es ist umstritten, ob man den Modernismus als klassische Bewegung ansehen darf. Die Modernisten waren offensichtlich dieser Ansicht, denn in seinem Aufsatz "Kommende Baukunst" (1923) vergleicht Le Corbusier die frühen Bauwerke, Brücken und Ozeandampfer mit griechischen Tempeln. Es fällt schwer, Mies van der Rohe, trotz seiner romantischen, visuellen Vorliebe, nicht im selben Licht zu sehen. Seine Tendenzen zur Reduzierung waren nicht ausschliesslich Inspiration des strukturellen Funktionalismus, sondern sein eingeborener Schönheitssinn überwindet immer blosse Funktionalität. Das Glaubensbekenntnis der Modernisten—"weniger ist mehr"— kann nur in seinem idealen Zusammenhang verstanden werden. Sogar Louis Kahn erscheint mit seiner Suche nach dem "was es sein will", und in seiner Leidenschaft für die Bewegung des Lichtes, klassisch—obwohl die Schwere seiner Werke ihnen auch romanische Züge verleiht.

Dem Klassizismus in der modernen Landschaftsarchitektur ist weniger einfach auf die Spur zu kommen. Man könnte berechtigterweise sagen, daß der Modernismus im Gartendesign sich lange nicht so verwirklicht hat, wie in dem von Bauwerken. Ich würde aber behaupten, daß Gärten lange vor der Architektur des 19. und 20. Jahrhunderts modern wurden, denn sowohl im traditionellen japanischen Garten, als auch in den formellen Anlagen des Franzosen André Le Notre im 17. Jahrhundert, sind nicht nur der wahre Geist des Klassizismus, sondern auch die Anfänge des Modernismus sichtbar.

Es ist schwierig, Beispiele klassischer Gartenbaupläne aus der Antike zu finden, außer als in Beschreibungen oder Zeichnungen. Es scheint keine formellen oder stilistischen Parallelerscheinungen zur klassischen Architekturordnung zu geben. Das heißt jedoch nicht, daß keine allgemeingültigen Richtlinien für Gärten existierten. Die Achsen, Alleen, Gebüsche, Bassins, Kanäle, Terrassen, Wege, Pflanzenbecken, Wiesen und Beete haben häufig wiederkehrende Komponenten klassischer und späterer Gärten mit Komponenten der Architektur gemein.

Klar scheint mir, daß der Garten objektiv als Element angesehen wurde, obschon fast immer als Teil der Architektur, definiert durch ein Gebäude, einen Säulengang oder eine Mauer. Weniger deutlich ist jedoch, wie man in der Antike die Landschaft im allgemeinen betrachtete, abgesehen vom künstlich angelegten Garten, vom Bauernhof, oder von landwirtschaftlichen Gebäuden, welche häufig aus Notwendigkeit sorgfältiger gepflegt wurden als heutige Gärten.

Meine Erfahrungen mit Gärten habe ich mir hauptsächlich durch intuitives Studium angeeignet, denn in Kontrast zur Wissenschaft sind Praxis und Lehre kein grundsätzlich geradliniges Unternehmen. Wie auch meinen zeitgenössischen Designern, war mir als Modernisten in den 50er Jahren ein integrierter Einblick in die Architekturgeschichte verwehrt, da unsere Professoren, einschließlich Gropius und Giedion und deren Anhänger, einen umfassenden historischen Überblick, die sie von ihren Lehrern erhalten hatten, nicht anboten. Damit haben sie die Möglichkeit unserer eigenen ideologischen Urteilskraft nicht gefördert. Auf Grund dessen fehlte mir die geschichtliche Perspektive, die der Fachmann vor 100 Jahren berechtigterweise erwartet hätte. Beispielsweise wurden die Ideen Corbusiers nicht zur Diskussion gestellt, weder daß der Ausdruck eines Gebäudes von innen, von seinem Plan, oder vom funktionellen Diagramm her komme, noch die vom architektonischen Objekt im Raum. Bis vor kurzem gab es im Modernismus wenig Debatte über die legitimen Ideen des Modernismus, oder über diejenigen, die man vielleicht hatte ausjäten sollen. Die stärkste Kritik am Modernismus besteht aus den Denunzierungen späterer Postmodernisten.

Die Abstraktion hat fast alles an Ausdrucks- und narrativen Elementen im modernen Design verdrängt. Bezugspunkte zur Natur in modernen Gebäuden fehlen im "internationalistischen"

Denken. Sozialer, demokratischer oder ökonomischer Nutzen hatte weitgehend die Metapher ersetzt, obwohl unklar war wie ein Dialog mit den Bewohnern erreicht werden konnte. Was jedoch "demokratisches Design" ohne diesen Dialog oder vereinbarte Richtlinien überhaupt sein sollte, ist mir bis heute nicht klar. Meine eigene Arbeit begann als Erforschung zweier Hauptthemen. Erstens, die Ausdehnung der Bauform, um eine Umgebung (sprich Sockel) für das kostbare Objekt, das Gebäude, zu schaffen. Zweitens, der Übergang von dieser Umgebung zu der sie umschliessenden, existierenden Landschaft. In den frühen 70er Jahren beunruhigten mich als Modernisten immer mehr die zunehmend lieblichen Tendenzen in meinen Arbeiten, die in scharfem Kontrast zu der minimalistischen Kunst der 60er Jahre standen, die ich zu der Zeit privat sammelte. Diese Kunstwerke schienen die Werke meiner Vorbilder, der frühen, modernistischen Architekten, besonders Mies van der Rohe, Louis Kahn und der Los Angeles "case study" Architekten der 50er Jahre, zu wiederspiegeln und fortzusetzen.

Die Arbeiten der Künstler Frank Stella, Carl Andre, Sol Lewitt, Donald Judd, Dan Flavin, Robert Morris und anderer der 60erJahre haben in meinen Augen die Einfachheit, die formale Kraft und Klarheit analytisch verstärkt und wiederbelebt, die der beste Teil meiner Studieneinführung in den Modernismus gewesen waren. Während dieser frühen Jahre sah ich keinerlei Beziehung zwischen Aspekten des historischen Klassizismus und den Unternehmungen des Modernismus, obwohl ich mit dem Vergleich Corbusiers zwischen griechischen Tempeln und Ozeandampfern vertraut war.

Um eine klassische und modernistische Arbeitstheorie der Landschaftsarchitektur zu entwickeln, sowohl akademisch als auch empirisch, habe ich zwei allgemeine Entwicklungsrichtungen der europäischen Landschaft während der klassischen Epoche untersucht. Die erste ist die hauptsächlich landwirtschaftliche Entwicklung in der nahen Umgebung von Dörfern und Stadtvororten. Diese waren durch das ganze 19. Jahrhundert hindurch für Persönlichkeiten wie John London und Thomas Jefferson ein Gegenstand kritischer Untersuchung. Der Hintergrund von architektonischen Gemälden und Portraits im frühen 19. Jahrhundert verändert sich von Wilder Natur zu bewirtschastetem Land. Landschaftsarchitektur beschäftigte sich in England und Amerika bis ins 20. Jahrhundert hinein mit landwirtschaftlichen Themen und bezog ästhetische Betrachtungen in seine Fragestellungen mit ein. Die andere Entwicklungsrichtung war die der architektonischen Ausdehnung. Mit dem Beginn des 15. Jahrhunderts wurden Außenräume hauptsächlich von Architekten mit Hilfe von Gärtnern entworfen. Im Allgemeinen nahmen sie die Form von Räumen, Terrassen, Treppen und Ornamenten an, die durch Steine, Pflaster und gestutzte Rankengewächse definiert wurden. Erst als im 18. Jahrhundert in Frankreich und England die Idee der Parkanlagen entstand, vermischten sich die architektonische und die landwirtschaftliche Denkrichtung. Zu diesem Zeitpunkt überrannte der malerische Aspekt die formalen oder geometrischen Entwicklungen der vergangenen 300 Jahre. Dem unerfahrenen Betrachter stellten sie sich nicht als Kunst, sondern als blosse Natur dar.

Die Lieblichkeit überschattete die Leistungen der grossartigen Schloßgärten und ganz besonders der Gärten von André Le Notre. Man ist der Auffassung, daß die englischen Gärten eher Ausdruck des Modernismus sind, da sie die "Natur" repräsentieren. Frederick Olmsted machte viel Wind um diese Idee und hielt sie in Bezug auf die Nachteile der industriellen Zivilisation für therapeutisch. In seinem Angriff auf französische und Renaissance-Gärten stützte sich Ian McHarg auf denselben Gedanken. Die französischen Gärten sind jedoch eher eine klassische Untersuchungsrichtung, da sie ganz klar die höchste Form von landwirtschaftlicher Entwicklung des 12. und 13. Jahrhunderts wiedergeben. Die Neuentwicklung der französischen (und später der englischen) landwirtschaftlichen Umgebung wurde durch die Verwaltungsmethoden der Kirche erreicht, die es anstrebte, den Bau ihrer Kathedralen mit der Bewirtschaftung der Umgebung zu finanzieren. In Le Notres Werken kann man ganz deutlich die Heckenreihen, Baumgruppen, künstlichen Teiche und die direkte Geometrie der französischen Landschaft erkennen. Sie sind sicherlich ebenso klassischer Ausdruck der Natur, wie die romantischeren, malerischen Gärten.

In Asien sah man den Garten als eigenständige Kunstform, völlig unabhängig von Architektur oder Landwirtschaft, und in seinem Wert und seiner Autonomie der Malerei, Bildhauerei, Musik und Dichtung ebenbürtig. Eine Formensprache und eine Vielseitigkeit von Ausdrucksmaßstäben wurde formuliert. In vieler Hinsicht verlief die Kultivierung und Verfeinerung dieser Gärten analog zu der der klassischen abendländischen Architektur.

Der Modernismus muß seine Artikulation der landschaftsarchitektonischen Theorie erst noch entwickeln, obwohl man in den wenigen Meisterwerken eine Untersuchung verschiedener formeller Methoden, abgeleitet von künstlerischen Stilen oder gar deren Kombination, wie Konstruktivismus oder Surrealismus, erkennen kann.

Mit Ausnahme der französischen Gartenbewegung in den 20er Jahren, hatten weder de Stijl, das Bauhaus, noch CIAM (Congrès Internationaux d'Architecture Moderne) die

Landschaftsarchitektur in grundsätzlicher oder prinzipieller Weise aufgegriffen. Ganz allgemein wurden offene Flächen und Natur als reichhaltigen und "leeren" Raum betrachtet, in welchen man Gebäude setzte, anstatt sie objektiv und qualitativ als Designfelder zu erkennen. Der offene Raum wurde in seiner Funktion, ähnlich der des weißen Würfels im modernen Ausstellungsgelände oder Kunstmuseum, als neutrale Umgebung verstanden. Bis heute haben die meisten Architekten eine ziemlich romantische Auffassung von der Landschaft als wilder Natur oder "weichem" Hintergrund. Die frühen modernistischen Architekten kamen in den späten 30er Jahren in England in den Vereinigten Staaten zum ersten Mal mit Lanschaftsarchitektur in Berührung, als Führende dieser Bewegung aus Europa flüchteten und in amerikanischen Universitäten zu lehren begannen.

Meine Arbeit der vergangenen 20 Jahre weist den Versuch auf, Elemente des Klassizismus, des europäischen und asiatischen Gartenformalismus und des Modernismus, einschließlich der Spätmodernisten und der Minimalisten der Mitte des Jahrhunderts, miteinander zu verflechten. Das Resultat ist das, was ich unter Minimalismus in der Landschaft verstehe.

Minimalismus in der Landschaft

Minimalismus in der Landschaft, abgesehen von seiner Definition in der Kunstwelt durch eine bestimmte Gruppe von Künstlern zu einem bestimmten Zeitpunkt in den 60er Jahren, scheint mir jenes Unterfangen der frühen Modernisten das wiederzubeleben, was in vielen Aspekten der Geist des Klassizismus in sich trägt. Die formelle Wiederentdeckung und Frage nach ursprünglicher Reinheit und menschlicher Bedeutung macht seine geistige Stärke aus: ein Interesse am Geheimnis und am bezugslosen Inhalt werden auf diese Weise mit klassischen Vorstellungen verbunden.

Wie auch der Begriff und die Idee des Klassizismus, ist der Minimalismus in unsere schnelllebige Gesellschaft getreten und von verschiedensten künstlerischen und kulturellen Disziplinen weiter und neu definiert worden. Im Grossen und Ganzen hält sich der Minimalismus an einer Methode, die jegliche Versuche ausschließt, Naturkräfte intellektuell, technisch oder industriell zu besiegen. Er schlägt das Konzept vor, die Realität natürlicher Systeme mit Geometrie, Erzählung, Rhythmus, Gestik und anderen Mitteln zu verändern, um den Raum mit einem Gefühl von Besonderheit zu beleben, das aber auf der Erinnerung basiert ist.

Trotz meiner weitgefaßten Anwendung des Begriffes Minimalismus, wird die Tendenz durch ein Beispiel auf einen wesentlichen minimalistischen Künstler anschaulich. Donald Judd bestand darauf, daß Minimalismus vornehmlich Ausdruck des Objektiven sei, Konzentration auf das Objekt selbst, statt auf Inhalt oder Interpretation. Minimalismus ist bezuglos und ist nicht repräsentativ, obwohl einige Betrachter unweigerlich ihre eigenen historischen oder ikonischen Vorstellungen hineinprojizieren. Obwohl die minimalistische Landschaft im Zusammenhang mit der Umgebung existiert, und obwohl sie Strategien der Unterbrechung und Interaktion beinhaltet und man an den geschaffenen Objekten vorbei in die Hintergrundslandschaft schaut, ist der Blickfang dennoch die gestaltete Landschaft, ihre Energie und ihr Raum. Die Größenordnung als Kontext und innere Erfahrung bleibt Hauptanliegen. Wie auch in der minimalistischen Kunst, ist die Landschaft des Minimalisten nicht unbedingt reduziert, obwohl diese Werke häufig minimale Komponenten und eine Direktheit besitzen, die Einfachheit impliziert.

Mit diesen Parametern eröffnet der Minimalismus in der Landschaftsarchitektur eine Infragestellung, die uns aufrütteln und durch die schwierigen Umstellungsphasen unserer Zeit führen kann: die Vereinfachung oder der Verlust handwerklicher Fertigkeiten, der Übergang von traditionellen, natürlichen zu synthetischen Materialien, und die Erweiterung menschlicher Maßstäbe zu den räumlichen und zeitlichen Übergrössen unseres maschinenbetriebenen modernen Lebens. In diesem Zusammenhang schlägt der Minimalismus einen künstlerisch erfolgreichen Ansatz zur Bewältigung der beiden kritischten Umweltprobleme vor: ansteigender Abfall und schwindende Rohstoffe.

Eine Beleuchtung des Minimalismus in der Landschaft scheint jetzt sehr zeitgemäß. Entwicklungen in der Landschaftsarchitektur, Architektur und Städteplanung während der sogenannten postmodernen Phase, stellen die Legitimität des modernistischen Designs in Frage, wobei mancher einen Rückzug auf den Klassizismus anstrebt. Viele der neueren Arbeiten und Gedanken auf diesem Gebiet haben sich einerseits mit formalen und dekorativen, andererseits mit soziologischen und funktionalen Themen befaßt. Minimalismus, eine Manifestation der letzten Züge des Hochmodernismus der visuellen Künste, hat selbst viele beeindruckende Verwandtschaften mit dem Klassizismus. Statt Entwurf und funktionelle Fragen als sich gegenseitig ausschließend zu verstehen, führt der Minimalismus zur Untersuchung des Abstrakten und des Wesentlichen; das sind Eigenschaften des klassischen als auch des modernistischen Designs.

Es ist nicht unwesentlich, daß der junge Corbusier, als er vor dem ersten Weltkrieg 1911 durch den Mittleren Osten und die Mittelmeerländer reiste, sich wegen der Qualität der Ruhe, des Lichtes und der einfachen, strengen Formen sehr von türkischen Moscheen, byzantinischen Klöstern und bulgarischen Häusern angezogen fühlte. Auf der Akropolis von Athen war er beim Anblick des Pantheon überwältigt und von Ehrfurcht gegenüber dem "unleugbaren Meisterwerk" erfüllt, das er später als Destillation von Form, als unübertroffenes Produkt der Maßstäblichkeit definierte. Er vermutete, daß ein Moment erreicht war, in dem nichts mehr mit weniger verbessert werden konnte. Ein Moment der Vollkommenheit, eine Definition des Klassischen. Es ergab sich, daß ich mit einem bestimmten Le Notre-Garten, den ich in den 70er Jahren besuchte, ein ähnliches Erlebnis hatte. Chantilly, ein grossartiger Steingarten aus Wasser, Raum und Licht ist ein hervorragendes Beispiel der auf Vollkommenheit reduzierter Form. Damals wie heute erscheint mir Chantilly eine Absicht in sich zu tragen, die sowohl klassisch als auch minimalistisch ist.

Diese Überlegungen sind gewissermaßen ein Entwicklungsbericht meines persönlichen Weges als Landschaftsarchitekt, der auf der Höhe des Modernismus im amerikanischen Landschaftsdesign zustande kam. Er ist durch Gärten, Landschaften, Designs, Künstler und Einblicke untermauert, die meine Wahrnehmungsfähigkeit geschult und meine Untersuchungsrichtung geleitet haben. Sie bieten eine persönliche Perspektive zur Schaffung von Umfeldern, die mir in heutiger Zeit sehr nötig erscheinen: Umfelder die ruhig und unbelastet sind, aber dennoch ausdrucksstark und bedeutungsvoll. Mehr denn je müssen wir in unsere bebaute Umgebung Sammelplätze eingliedern, müssen Funktionalität mit Raum für Entdeckung, Rückzug und Stille vereinbaren in dem zunehmend verwirrenden, geistig verarmten, vollgestopften und ungepflegten Garten unserer Erde.

Die Kunst ist kein Garten

Mein Übergang vom bloßen Kunstliebhaber zum selbstbewußten Landschaftsarchitekten, der abstrakte Ideen in seine Kunst zu integrieren versucht, geschah nur sehr schleppend. Zunächst stöberte ich als Sammler in Galerien und las mit Heißhunger Bücher, Kunstzeitschriften und -kataloge, besonders über die Minimalisten. Ich war mir keines beruflichen Interesses, noch irgendwelcher überlappender Denkprozesse bewußt, sondern nur der Neugierde auf die Schönheit und Bedeutung der Kunst und der visuellen und geistigen Energien, die diese erzeugte.

Ich erinnere mich, daß mir nach einigen Jahren etwas in Frank Stellas frühen Streifenbildern auffiel, das ich als landschaftarchitektonische Inspiration aufgriff: das innere Wesen der Muster definiere die Gestalt eines zweidimensionalen Gemäldes, ersetze den Rahmen, und schließe die Möglichkeit als Abstraktion verstanden zu werden aus. Dies war also wie ein Garten ohne Mauern, fähig in räumlichem Zusammenhang zu existieren und gleichzeitig selbst Objekt zu sein.

Dann begannen mir die von von Carl Andres geschaffenen Bodenskulpturen aus Metall mir als deutliche Metaphern für Gärten aufzufallen: alle auf flacher Ebene und fast keinerlei Dreidimensionalität und dennoch beherrschten sie das Wesen des "leeren" Raumes über ihnen. Sie erinnerten mich an die Perserteppiche der Wüstenbeduinen: bewegliche, ideale und intime Gärten. Eine weitere Arbeit von Andre, "144 Blöcke und Steine", aus dem Jahr 1973 wurde durch diese Interpretation ganz besonders dynamisch. Zu ihrer Installation wurden alle Wände der Galerie (sprich Architektur) geräumt und der Boden (sprich Landschaft) wurde zu einem komplexen und geheimnisvollen Totem oder Spiel. Die Materialien waren bescheiden, sogar gewöhnlich, aber das Ergebnis war äußerst ansprechend, und ich erlebte eine starke Verbindung zwischen den geheimnisvollen Kräften der Kunst und denen der Gartenkunst.

Eine weitere Arbeit von Andre, "Secant", (1977) war in einer gewöhnlichen Wiese aufgebaut. Die Wiese hatte ihre natürliche Schönheit, unterschied sich aber nicht weiter von tausend anderen in der Umgebung. Indem Andre auf eindeutig einfache Weise eine Reihe abgefällter Bäume auf sie plazierte, verwandelte sie in einen Ort, der bewußte und unterbewußte Erinnerungen erweckte.

In ähnlicher Weise war Christos "Running Fence" 1972-76 in einer gewöhnlichen Landschaft westwärts zum Pazifischen Ozean rollender Hügel in den Marin und Sonoma Counties von Kalifornien gebaut worden und belebte diese Landschaft zu einem Niveau der hohen Feierlichkeit. Ich war in eben jenen küstennahen Hügeln aufgewachsen und hatte fast immer dort gelebt und meinte sie besser zu kennen, als die meisten Menschen, auf jeden Fall besser als jegliche andere Landschaft, die ich je betreten hatte. Dennoch hatte ich sie noch nie so wahrgenommen oder mich ihr so verbunden gefühlt. Es war überwältigend, daß ein Zaun aus Seidentüchern solch ein Erkennen hervorrufen konnte. Zu jener Zeit begriff ich jedoch die direkte Beziehung zwischen meinem Angesprochensein und meiner Begeisterung als Betrachter und dem, was ich als Landschaftsarchitekt erdacht und erstellt hatte noch nicht.

Mit der Zeit unterstützten und erweiterten immer mehr Kunstwerke mein steigendes Interesse am Potential der Integration von Kunst und Architektur, und schließlich wurde ich des bloßen Kunstsammelns überdrüssig. Nach einer Sommerreise durch französische Gärten in den späten 70er Jahren kristallisierte sich die Verbindung zwischen den großen, historischen, formellen

Gärten, der minimalistischen Kunst und meiner eigenen Vision von Landschaftsarchitektur, und ich begann neue Wege der Gartengestaltung auszuprobieren. Die ersten Versuche waren recht vorsichtig. Es wurde mir schnell klar, daß die einfache Übertragung einer künstlerischen Idee, inspiriert durch ein Werk in einer Galerie oder an einem speziellen Ort, weder eine erfolgreiche Strategie noch eine neue Richtung in der Landschaftsarchitektur ausmachte, da die anderen Dimensionen der Natur zunächst noch miteinbezogen werden mußten.

Obwohl der Begriff der Objektivierung nützlich war, konnte die Idee, einen Sinn zu manifestieren nicht von anderen dringenden Faktoren isoliert werden. Objekte und formale Systeme werden in der gestalteten Landschaft in starkem Kontrast zum größeren Umfeld empfunden, welches nicht nur die besonderen Eigenschaften des gewählten Raumes und seiner Umgebung beinhaltet, sondern, um weiter auszugreifen, auch den Rhythmus des täglichen Kreislaufs der Sonne und des Mondes, die Veränderung des jahreszeitlich bedingten Lichtes und des Klimas, und ganz besonders die extremen Naturerscheinungen und die eher zufälligen Charakteristiken von Entstehung, Wachstum und Zerfall. Dieses komplexe Zusammenspiel der Natur mit dem einfachsten, hinzugefügten beziehungsweise plazierten Objekt verdeutlicht und verstärkt die für diese Arbeit in der Landschaft nötige Erwartungshaltung, wobei die Zeit ein ebenso wichtiger Faktor wie der Raum ist.

Obwohl mir diese Erkenntnis seinerzeit in ihrer Klarheit neu war, ist sie doch offensichtlich. Auf dem Gebiet der heutigen Landschaftsarchitektur werden das Element der Zeit und dieTatsache der Unvorhersehbarkeit in ihrer Wichtigkeit nicht genügend betont, und zwar aus drei hauptsächlich kartesischen Gründen. Zunächst dominiert noch immer eine wissenschaftlich-technologische Tendenz, das Geheimnis der Natur zu zerlegen, zu bewältigen und zu beherrschen, anstatt jenes Geheimnis zu ehren. Weiterhin bleibt die Unfähigkeit bestehen, sich mit der verzweigten Buntheit und Veränderbarkeit in der Natur auseinanderzusetzen, während man sich auf das Ziel konzentriert, die "höchste" Leistung zu bringen. (Vielleicht hat die Wiedererkennbarkeit einen zu hohen Rang in unserem Wertsystem inne). Und schließlich besteht eine Überbetonung des Details und der spezifischen Ausführung, die aus einer fraglichen Quelle der modernistischen Schule der Architektur stammt.

Wenn die Devise zutreffen soll, "die Form folgt der Funktion", dann wird es Priorität, die Funktion zu analysieren, damit die Form ihr folgt. Die Form drückt die Funktion als Erfolgsmaßstab für Designziele aus. Die einfühlsamere und künstlerische Herangehensweise des Entwerfens in und mit der Natur, und anfangs auch der verallgemeinerte und universale Plan, legt die wunderbaren Eigenschaften und Zukunftsmöglichkeiten offen, die in dem Wechselspiel zwischen menschlichem, physischem Schaffen und der sich ständig verändernden Welt der Natur liegt. Das eigentliche Problem mit meiner Konzeption von Landschaftsarchitektur war, daß ich zwar einen Überfluß an grundsätzlichen Ideen besaß, daß aber die Richtlinien zur Auswahl derer, die sich tatsächlich als brauchbar, bedeutungsvoll, schön und sogar geheimnisvoll oder spirituell erweisen würden, noch sehr vage waren.

Die unwahrscheinliche Verbindung des Denkens und der Kunst der Minimalisten mit den Bedingungen des offenen Raumes, von zeitgenössischen Landschaftsarchitekten noch nicht wahrgenommen, eröffnete einen faszinierenden und herausfordernden Weg der Untersuchung und des Experimentierens. Das Problem auf diese Weise anzugehen, sich mit allen Aspekten der Umgebung auseinanderzusetzen (verödetes Land, verlassene Strassen, Parkplätze und Dächer miteinbeschlossen), als auch der traditionelleren Beschäftigung mit Gärten, Parkanlagen und verschiedenen Arten von Plätzen) ist eine neue Einsicht. Sie liefert die Basis, unser Städte und Vorstädte, sowohl alte als neue, mit neuen Augen zu betrachten.

Sichtbarkeit

Um wirklich erkennbar zu sein, muß ein Objekt, zumindest teilweise, für sich allein gesehen werden. Wenn eine Arbeit größtenteils seiner Umgebung untergeordnet oder mit der bestehenden Ordnung verwechselt wird, ist ihr die Möglichkeit des Ausdrucks, der Bedeutung des Narrativen oder des Einflusses auf die Erinnerung genommen. Sogar hervorragendes Dekor kann keine bewußte Wahrnehmung erzeugen, wenn es neben anderen vorhandenen, künstlerischen Erscheinungsformen als Objekt nicht bestehen kann.

Die moderne Gesellschaft ist fragmentiert und kommerziell. Die Landschaft wird als offen und leer gesehen und vieles im modernen städtischen Raum ist sozusagen Überbleibsel, am Rande der Vernachlässigung. Symbole der Feierlichkeit verschwinden zusehends. Natürliche, geschichtliche und entfremdete Bilder ersetzen immer mehr das echte Naturerlebnis. Was bietet sich unter diesen Umständen als Strategie zur Sichtbarkeit an?

Physische Unterteilungen haben die Tendenz, unseren Sinn für die natürliche Ordnung zu vermindern. Bäche werden unterbrochen und in Röhren geleitet, man schneidet in Hügel und

Berge hinein, verschiebt sie oder verunstaltet sie fürs Auge. Bürgersteige werden für unnötig gehalten. Gebäude und chemische Verunreinigung blockieren den natürlichen Verlauf des Geländes, einschliesslich des Meeres und sogar des Himmels. Natürliche, beeindruckende Landschaftseinheiten, wie zum Beispiel das Los Angeles Basin, die Insel von Manhattan, der Charles River bei Boston und ein lange Reihe anderer Beispiele, sind von durch Menschenhand gestaltete Straßen, Autobahnen, Gebäuden (und teilweise auch künstlichen Landschaften), visuell geschwächt worden.

Diesen Mutationen liegt ein abnehmender Sinn für Ordnung, Ruhe und visuelle Dimension zugrunde, als auch der Verlust der Stabilität, die der Mensch der prämodernen Zeit in Bergen, Ebenen, Seen, Flüssen und Meeren, landwirtschaftlichen Flecken und Dörfern und kleinen Städten fand. All jene Momente reflektierten die Größe der Natur, die eine Beziehung zur Erde als Ganzes herstellte.

Wenn einfache Ordnung in starkem Kontrast zur Fragmentation, Eingrenzung und Unterbrechung steht, bieten die Werte der Reduktion und der Konzentration eine Richtung für unsere Kultur. Häufig angewandte Formelemente in der minimalistischen Kunst und in traditionellen, formalen Gärten sind Serienmäßigkeit und Wiederholung, Geometrie (besonders lineare und punktierte Planquadrate), wahrnehmbare Ausdehnung der Dimension, lineare Gestik und die visuelle Ausnutzung der Kanten und Zentren einschließlich bilateraler und assymetrischer Symetrie. Die Ausschöpfung der Oberflächenstruktur und des Musters, der Skala und des Farbkontrastes, als auch des Synthetischen gegenüber dem Natürlichen, des Lebendigen gegenüber dem Erstarrten, sind ebenfalls Ordnungsrichtlinien in diesem Zusammenhang. Dieser Liste kann noch Feierlichkeit, Erzählung und Symbol hinzugefügt werden. In der Absicht, die Analyse auf wesentliche, visuelle Eigenschaften zurückzuleiten ist das Ziel letztendlich, Mysterium statt Ironie zu schaffen.

Landschaft als Kunst

Der offene Raum ist im öffentlichen, kulturellen und modernen, sozialen Leben von ebenso großer, wenn nicht sogar von größerer Bedeutung als der Innenraum. Die entworfene Landschaft kann ebenso feierlichen Ausdruck oder auch Rätsel enthalten, wie eine jegliche Fassade oder andere architektonische Form oder Dimension. Die öffentlichen Orte, die ausschließlich zweckmässig aus der Funktion entstehen, angefüllt mit nützlichen, aber der Schönheit beraubten Straßen, Parkplätzen und Tankstellen, tragen eine gleichgültige Häßlichkeit in sich und trüben damit die Hoffnungen des Modernismus in dem Maße, daß er tatsächlich als gescheitert empfunden wird. Ein großer Teil dieses Versagens liegt in der Städteplanung und den öffentlichen Anlagen der Groß- und Kleinstädte.

Eines der Themen der klassischen Architektur ist der Rückgriff auf die Natur und die Suche nach dem klassischen Ideal durch Generationen der Erfindung, der Neuinterpretation, der Wiedergabe und Verflechtung dieser Themen mit denen einer sich ständig erweiternden und bereichernden Kultur. Wie kann man parallel dazu eine Kunstform betrachten, die in sich selbst größtenteils Natur ist? Ich vermute die Antwort liegt in der Fähigkeit, die Natur in ihren zwei Erscheinungsformen zu sehen, der wilden und der gezähmten.

Wilde Natur und Landschaft befinden sich nie in einem Stadium der Stabilität oder Dauer, wie das die klassische Architektur voraussetzt. Daher ist die Architektur eine hinkende Analogie für die Landschaftsthematik. Obwohl die Musik häufig benutzt wird, um Landschaft zu beschreiben, ist sie zu vergänglich, und trotz musiaklische Beschreibungen der Räumlichkeit (siehe die Werke von John Cage), ist sie nicht wie der Raum, physisch betretbar. Der offene Raum ist ein sehr komplexes Medium in seiner Abhängigkeit vom ständigen Wechsel der täglichen, jahreszeitlichen und der Reifungszyklen, verkompliziert durch Geräusch, Geruch, Temperatur und Niederschlag. Verglichen mit allen anderen Medien der Kunst kommt er der Vielschichtigkeit des menschlichen Daseins am nächsten.

Eine sich ständig verändernde Natur ermöglicht eine außerordentliche Kunstform, einzigartig und separat von allen anderen. Die vorhandenen Kriterien sind noch immer im Entwicklungsstadium, offen für Erweiterung, Diskussion, Möglichkeiten, Richtungsfindung und Hoffnung.

Viele Fragen müssen in Betracht gezogen werden: Ist diese Landschaft zu wild? Kann die moderne Landschaft (natürlich oder städtisch) ausreichend bemeistert werden, um Kontext und Inhalt einer Kunstform zu sein? Kann eine Landschaftskonzeption genügend Ordnung in der Vielseitigkeit der modernen Existenz schaffen? Können unsere Mittel, anders ausgedrückt, den angestrebten Zweck erreichen? Ich glaube daran und sehe Zeichen des Erfolges in den innovativen Arbeiten von Louis Barragan, Isamu Noguchi, Roberto Burle Max, Dan Kiley, Lawrence Halprin und anderen großen Landschaftsarchitekten unserer Zeit. Für mich ist der Minimalismus eine Untersuchungsrichtung, die uns das breite Spektrum der Lösungen eröffnet, das unsere Kultur erwartet.

ピーター・ウォーカーのランドスケープ

リア・レヴィー
訳／長谷川浩己

現代において、いわゆるデザインされたランドスケープという対象は、一貫して建築と一体に扱われてきたことは明らかであろう。ランドスケープ「アーキテクト」の仕事は建築家（アーキテクト）のデザインする建造物の周辺またはそれらの間のスペースの修景へと押しやられ、あらかじめ与えられた空間のなかに人目を引く造形を提供してきたにすぎない。大学カリキュラムの中でのランドスケープ・デザインの領域はかつての農学、園芸学から、現在は建築と同じ学科で扱われている。ここに私たちが考えねばならない重要なことが一つある。かつてランドスケープ・デザインと庭園デザインについて積み重ねられてきた議論が今後どう展開されるべきか。例えば、それは建築学の一環なのか、それとも農学系の話なのだろうか。

ピーター・ウォーカーというランドスケープ・アーキテクトの作品を語る場合、今までのランドスケープ・デザインと庭園デザインの評価基準にはとうてい収まりきらない。彼は特定の「場」に根ざしたランドスケープ・デザインを他の視覚芸術や舞台芸術、そして建築と並ぶ独立した領域とみなし、風景を視覚化することに力を注いできた。もっともランドスケープ・デザインについての評論は、いまだ他の芸術分野に比して質、量ともあまりにも貧弱であるのが実状だが。

ところで実はこんなところに彼のスタイルのルーツの一端が見られるのではないだろうか。ペルーのナスカの地上絵、イギリスのストーン・ヘンジ、これら地上に描かれた古代の遺跡は、土地の上に私たちの痕跡を残そうという最も根源的な、そして人類共通の衝動を今に伝えている。一見全く何の関係もないようだがそこには彼の思想と相通ずるものが確かに感じられよう。自分たちを取りまくより大きな存在とつながりたいという抗い難い欲求、地上の、そして天上の神秘への探求、強大なる力への言及、彼の作品にはこうした流れが明らかに感じられる。水の音、石の静謐とその重量感、風のざわめき、様々な色彩のパターン、おぼろげに揺らめく霧、うつろう光など、多くの作品の中にその流れは姿を現わす。

同様にル・ノートルに代表される17世紀フランスの古典庭園は、ウォーカーの個人的姿勢の大きな拠り所の一つとなっている。彼の直観的かつ知性的な、パターン、リズム、秩序、またはある種のデカルト的統合への嗜好は全ての作品を通じて明らかである。

また日本の禅寺における庭園様式も彼に大きな影響を与えた。複雑な事象は哲学的純化を通して、限りなくシンプルな形態へと昇華する。その思想は明瞭なデザイン要素として、また空間全てを支配する底流として、彼のデザインした庭園の中に見え隠れしている。

彼の成し遂げてきた仕事はたしかに現代ランドスケープ・デザインの歴史の中に大きな位置を占めている。ひとりのデザイナーとして、彼は一貫して20世紀のランドスケープ・デザインの歴史に敬意をはらい、その歴史の一翼を担ってきた。1　特に20世紀中葉に活躍したトーマス・チャーチとイサム・ノグチの数々の作品が、彼のスタイル形成の時期において大きな影響を与えたのは事実である。しかし今日の文化的コンテクストの中で何にもましてウォーカーのランドスケープの意味を理解するのに最も適しているアプローチは、現代文化の中での彼の作品の位置づけ、各芸術分野をめぐる彼自身の考察、また今世紀における主要な芸術運動の分析などを通してではないだろうか。

20世紀初頭は芸術のみならず、科学、文化の面でも新しい世紀の道筋をつけようという創造的エネルギーで満ちあふれていた時代であった。視覚芸術の世界では、純粋抽象芸術が新しい知覚の領域を切り開くものとして登場した。芸術はもはや現実を参照、模倣することなく、それ自身自立した抽象的形態の追求が表現と探求の手段となった。幾何学的形態をベースにした作品の多くを通して、特に初期のロシア構成主義者たちは更に直接的な関係を求めてやまなかった。人類がその歴史を通じて追い求めてきた普遍なるものの神秘を明らかにし、描き出すために。それはそれまでの現実的規範の範疇ではとうてい説明し得ない「個人的対象としての現象」を熟視し、理解するための手法であった。

固定化してしまった歴史の楔から解き放たれて2次元の平面、3次元の空間芸術はあたかも音楽のように振る舞い始めた。特定の、それと分かる事象を再生産するのではなく、あくまでも自立したそのもの自身を創造する。この新しい自由を得て、アーティストと観客たちは共に意識を超えたレベルへと歩を進めていくことが可能となったのである。

20世紀初頭における独創的精神のもう一つの例はフランスのアーティスト、マルセル・デュシャンの作品であろう。彼はオブジェ（現実のものであれ抽象的イメージであれ）に審美性、意味づけを見いだすことを拒否し、単なる視覚の世界を超えて精神の領域にまで踏み込んだ。そうして「何が芸術たるかを規定するのはアーティスト自身である」との宣言の下に、デュシャンは芸術的実践の対象を次々と拡大してみせたのである。芸術作品の位置づけを曖昧にし、まるで芸術作品とは思えないような雑多なものまで彼のアイデアと共に作品として扱うことにより、彼は従来の絵画や彫刻を超え、今日へと続く新たな芸術の領域を開拓する事に成功したといえる。

社会、政治、文化的状況の変化一段と進むなか、抽象表現主義のみならずデュシャンの前衛的

理論を背景にミニマリズムの萌芽の時がやってきた。最も重要な時期であった1960年代以降、ミニマリズムは真の意味でアメリカから全世界へ向けられた最初の芸術運動と目されるまでになる。その言葉は広く社会に浸透し、非形態的、非参照的態度、幾何学的形態の使用のみならず単にシンプルな構成や材料からなるものまでほとんど脈絡なくミニマリズムと呼ばれるまでにいたったのである。

しかし実際のところミニマリズムという単語は、1963年から1968年にかけてドナルド・ジャッド、ダン・フレイビン、ソル・ルイット、ロバート・モリス、カール・アンドレなど主にニューヨークを拠点としたごく限られた作家によって標榜されたものだった。彼らの作品はそれまでの芸術形態の範疇にいれられることを拒否し、新しい哲学的基盤の上に立っていた。作家たちの目指したところはたとえば「空間の中に確固として存在し、同じくそこに存在する観客との身体的距離の近さによってのみ認知可能なオブジェの創造」2、または「その時、その場限りの非再生型コミュニケーション」3　などが挙げられる。また特定の場所におけるマテリアルそのものが発する存在感は、観客に直接訴えかける力を内在するとされた。そしてリアルな身体的体験の対象としてのマテリアルはミニマル・アートの主題をなし、作家にとって決して欠かすことのできないテーマとなった。こうして最も直接的に根源的経験を生み出すようなシンプルなオブジェへの道を探し求めて、ミニマル・アーティストたちは次第に最大の効果を生むべく逆に抑制的な方向へと傾いていったのである。

この新しいアートの本質は観客から見た「オブジェとそれが置かれた環境との相互作用」であったから、これら一連の作品はややもすると単なるフォルマリズムと混同された。作品はその色、かたち、大きさなどについては容易に描写が可能だが、しかしその場を実際に歩き、通り抜け、そばに佇み、そして中に入り込むことなくしては決して説明がつかない。確かにフォルマリズム的な色合い（それはしかし常に変化するものでもある）も見受けられるが、単純に幾何学的形態の使用、オブジェの反復、システム的配置、工業製品や現代特有の素材の使用、立体（彫刻とは一線を画すが）、原色の使用などがミニマル・アートの特徴である。また重要なもう一つの特徴は、台座を排し作品を直接床に置いたり額縁を取り去って壁に直接立てかけることにより、空間との関係をより直接的に実現しようとしたことにある。

ここで忘れてはならない重要な点をもう一つ指摘しておきたい。ミニマル・アートにおいてはその作品がどこに置かれ、どう見られるのかが極めて重要だということである。この作品は例えばギャラリーの白い箱を想定したものなのか、または屋外での展示になるのか。アーティストは彼の作品、私たち観客の身体性、そしてそれが置かれる空間の物理的、現象学的関係の成立をもくろみ、そのうえで空間内に己存在する全てのエレメントの相関的スケールは慎重に計算され、決定されるのである。

20世紀文化を表現、具現化する美学的根拠としてのフォルマリズムの感性は、ミニマリストたちによって実践された。彼らの美意識への共感のみならず、ピーター・ウォーカーの作品は20世紀を代表する他の芸術分野への大きな関心をも示している。ここに一団のアーティストたちがいる。そのフォルムの規則的な抽象性からしばしばミニマリズムとして扱われたが、その根底には彼ら独特の違った哲学的根拠がしっかりと裏付けられていた。彼らの中には造形家と共に画家も含まれており、主なアーティストとしてアド・ラインハート、アグネス・マーティン、ロバート・ライマン、ロバート・マンゴールド、エルスウォース・ケリー、ポルフィリオ・ディドナ、イブ・クライン、ジャスパー・ジョーンズ、ロバート・アーウィンなどが挙げられる。彼らが行なった抽象化はもっと潜在的な意識下の世界の探求であり、その意味を探る試みであった。これらの作品に見られるリズムや反復するパターンは、ミニマル・アートにおける無差別的、相対的規則性を実現させるための機構としてというよりは、有機体のシステム（たとえば潮の満ち引きや心臓の鼓動などの儀式的ともいえる運動性）や詩の韻律に近いものがあろう。

もう一つ現代アートの領域の中で、ランド・アーティスト、またはアース・アーティストと呼ばれ、主に広大かつ多様なプロジェクトを戸外の環境で行なってきた人たちがいる。このタイトルから分かるように彼らは何の必然性も具体的目的も持たず、純粋に「自然」と交感するために広大無辺の大地を相手にしてきた（例えばロバート・スミッソンの螺旋型の突堤、ウォルター・デ・マリアの大地への操作、マイケル・ハイザーの大地と岩の造型、それにデニス・オッペンハイムとロバート・モリスの作品など）。またある作家たちは意識的に環境と人類の関わり方について言及し、時にはそれは自然に対する一編の詩として制作された。アンディ・ゴールドワージーの氷の造型や繊細な小枝の作品、天体の運行を祝福するためにジェームズ・タレルが手を加えている死火山のクレーター、ナンシー・ホルトの光を内にはらんだトンネル、またイアン・ハミルトン・フィンレイの古典的作庭やリチャード・フライシュナーの彫刻的ランドスケープなどがその例として挙げられるだろう。

今までに挙げた作家だけでなくその他実に様々な作家（シャー・アルマジャーニ、ダグラス・ホリス、マヤ・リン、リチャード・セラ、アリス・エイコック、クリストなど）の関心はいわゆる大自然だけでなく、より公共的な都市のランドスケープをも視野に入れてきつつある。またドナルド・ジャッドの建造物、デイビッド・アイルランドの家屋や壁のインスタレーション、ゴードン・マッタークラークの断片化した建築エレメント、スコット・バートンの都市内の家具な

ど、ある者は建築的デザインやインスタレーションにまで踏み込んできた。これらの作品のいくつかは洗練された現代的ビジョンを提示しようとし、しかしまたある作品は反対に、積み上げられた石、水のほとばしりといった極めて初源的なモチーフを都市に持ち込むことにより、自然の神秘や言葉を超えた自然の輝きを映し出そうとしている。

ピーター・ウォーカーの作品は以上述べてきた様々な芸術運動スタイルからその影響を受けているが、同時に今世紀のアートシーンにおける本質を彼自身が追求して来た結果の集大成でもある。彼のスタイルは彼独自のビジョンと特定の「場所性」とが統合された結果であり、それは今までのどのカテゴリーにも属さないものである。そこで私たちも彼が自らを名乗るのにならって、ランドスケープ・デザイナーという独立した領域を認めるに至ったのである。彼の作品にはミニマリズムとの密接な関係が見られるがそれは決して彼が芸術史上の重要な様式を単にまねして再現しているのではなく、ミニマリズムの視覚的、精神的ボキャブラリーがウォーカーの作品の本質的な部分に深く関わっているからである。

自然を探求し、明らかにするための手段としてピーター・ウォーカーは抽象的、連続的、そして幾何学的表現の価値への強い意志を持ち続けてきたが、彼はまた同時にランドスケープ・デザインの重要なコンテクストの一つとして現代アートの実用的、政治的性格を認めてきた。個々のミニマル・アート、そしてアースワークの実践はオブジェと風景の関係を見えるものにし、そこでの「場所性」の存在や位置づけを訴えかける。そして大地の上に働きかけることの意義を拡張し、より深い理解へと私たちを導く。美の追求もさることながら、ピーター・ウォーカーはユーモア、批評精神、解体作業、洒落、議論、協働、そして詩という存在を忘れることがない。ピーター・ウォーカーのいうランドスケープ・デザインとは、個人的、専門的、芸術的、などという固定観念を超え、実に私たちの住む環境をどうとらえるのかということを探る試みそのものである。私たちはこの地球という惑星と共に一体何を築き上げることが出来るのか。最終的に目指すべきゴールとはこういうことではあるまいか。

1 Peter Walker と Melanie Simo, *Invisible Gardens: The Search for Modernism in the American Landscape* (Cambridge: Massachusetts Institute of Technology Press, 1994).

2 Frances Colpitt, *Minimal Art: The Critical Perspective* (Seattle: University of Washington Press, 1993).

3 Maurice Tuchman, その他, *The Spiritual in Art: Abstract Painting, 1890-1985* (New York: Abbeville Press, 1986).

4 John Beardsley, *Earthworks and Beyond: Contemporary Art in the Landscape* (New York: Abbeville Press, 1989).

ランドスケープ・デザインにおける古典主義、モダニズム、ミニマリズム

ピーター・ウォーカー
訳／長谷川浩己

古典主義、そしてモダニズム

古典主義とは古典主義者にとっては、いうまでもなく文字どおり古代ギリシャ、その復古主義、古代ローマについての学問である。ただそれぞれの時代の美術史家、芸術家、建築家はその時代の要請に会うように古典主義という言葉を再定義してきた。たとえば復古主義、新古典主義など様々なカテゴリーで名付けられ、良し悪しを判定され、絵画、彫刻、音楽、文学、建築など多くの分野でそれぞれに折衷的な解釈が成されてきた。

しかしながらそれらの解釈の多くは明白さ、純粋性、人間性の表現、自然界からの引用、工芸または建築技術からの表現的引用など、古典主義的理想の中に見え隠れする共通項についての一般的合意に過ぎないように思える。だとすれば私の求める古典主義の持つある精神的な質については、これらの多岐にわたる解釈をあたるよりも作品そのものか、もしくは古典主義の時代そのものに焦点を当てた方がずっと考察しやすいのではないだろうか。

モダニズムは果たして古典主義運動なのか（または、であったのか）。これはとても興味深い議論となり得る。明らかに初期モダニストはそう考えたであろう。「建築をめざして」の中でル・コルビュジエは古代の偉大な土木技術、橋梁、大洋を航る商船、そしてギリシャの寺院を並列に論じている。そして私はミース・ファン・デ・ローエの作品にも同じ傾向を認めざるを得ない。たとえ彼がいかにロマン主義への傾倒を公然と語っていたにしても。また如何に彼の抑制的な態度が必ずしも構造機能的発想を基にしたものではないにしても、である。美のあるべき姿とは、常に単なる必要性を越えたところにあると私は考える。モダニストの金科玉条である 'Less is more' もこのコンテクストにおいてのみ意義を持つと言うべきだろう。ルイス・カーンの表現する量感がロマネスクの影響を受けていることは間違いないにしても、彼の追求した「それが何であろうとしているのか」という問題、そして彼が情熱を傾けた光のうつろいのデザインもまた同様に古典的であるといえるのではないだろうか。

現代のランドスケープ・デザインの中における古典主義の位置づけについて、建築と同列に論じるのはちょっと無理があるかもしれない。率直に言えばモダニズムそのものさえ建築の世界のように理解されているとはいいがたいからだ。しかし私は次の点を強調したい。すなわち19世紀末から20世紀に掛けて建築の世界でモダニズムが語られるようになる遥か以前に日本やル・ノートルの庭園は既にモダンであったということを。それらの庭園は古典主義の真髄を具現していただけでなく、モダニズムの始まりでもあったことは明らかである。

今日、古代ギリシャ、ローマの庭園についてはその描写されたものを除いては現存していない。ただおそらく古典建築的オーダーから導かれるようなフォーマルなものではなかったようである。しかし、だからといって庭園を構成する数々のデザイン言語が存在しなかったということを意味しているわけではない。見晴らし台、手すり、階段、斜路など建築的要素と共に、軸線、小道、ボスク、水盤、水路、テラス、歩道、パスティーユ、草原などの庭園的要素もまた古典様式であり、後の庭園にもよく用いられた。

ほとんどの庭園は建物の一部として壁面や柱廊によって規定された空間であったが、しかし同時に一つの独立した要素として認識されていたのもまた事実である。ただその時代においてどうであったのか、次の点についてはどうもはっきりしない。デザインされた庭園は、果たしてその外に広がる風景とは切り放されて独立した主体として認識されていたのだろうか。またその当時、今日の庭よりよほど丁寧に造りこまれていた農地も同様に、周囲からは自立した空間だったのだろうか。

ところで私自身について言えば、庭園についてのほとんどを直観的な探求を通して学んできた。私は学術的分野に身をおいてきたわけでもないし、学校での教授の仕事も基本的には時系列に沿ってきちんと行なってきたものではないからだ。1950年代に教育を受けたモダニスト第二世代として、私を含め当時の多くの建築家は一貫した建築史の流れを教えてもらうことができなかった。グロピウス、ギーディオンをはじめとする教授陣は彼ら自身が学生時代に教わったような十分な歴史的事実を私たちへ伝えようとはしなかった。彼らは学生たちが自らそのイデオロギーを選びとることを望まなかったのであろうか。ともあれそういった訳で私自身、100年前普通に教育を受けたデザイナーが持っていたであろう歴史的視野を持ち合わせていない。当時モダニズムは唯一のイデオロギーであった。例えば建築的表現はその内面、平面、機能的ダイアグラムからこそ立ち現れるというル・コルビジェの考え、または空間の中における建築的存在についての彼の考察、などが疑問や議論の対象になることはついぞなかった。たとえ彼の考え方の限界性がいかに明らかなものであったとしてもだ。つい最近になるまでモダニズムという思想に対して十分な議論や理論的な洗練を図ることはほとんど行われず、モダニズムの持つ本当の正当性は、その他の取捨選択されるべき雑多な定義付けと混同されたままであった。ここに来てようやくモダニズムへの批判が噴き出しているが、批判の大半はいわゆるポスト・モダン的立場から弾

効の形をとって行われているに過ぎない。

抽象化の流れはモダニズムのデザインからコンテクストの表出と物語性を排除してきた。そしてインターナショナリズム的思考によって、固有の自然への言及もまた現代建築から抜け落ちてきた。社会的、民主的、経済的要請がメタファーにとって替わり、建築と利用者との間の対話をどうやって実現させるか、という事は二の次にされてきたのである。しかしこの対話無しにはたとえいかに言葉で取り繕ったとしても、モダニストが唱えた民主的デザインとは一体何なのか、私には疑わしいものに思えてならない。

私自身の探求は2つの主要なテーマの追求から始まった。建築と調和し得る外部環境の状況を創出するために建築の形態を延長してみる、そして次にそのデザインされた状況から周辺の既存の風景へと続く移行部分の仕上げをどう決めるか、ということであった。

1970年始めまでに私自身の作風は次第にピクチャレスク的傾向のデザインに傾いていったが、実のところそれは同じ頃個人的に収集していた60年代のミニマル・アートとはあまりにもはっきりとした対極にあった。ただそれら収集されたアートのなかに私のヒーローである初期モダニスト達すなわちミース、カーン、そして50年代ロスアンジェルスの実験的な建築家の作に何か通ずるものを感じていたようには思う。

フランク・ステラ、カール・アンドレ・ソル・ルイット、ドナルド・ジャッド、ダン・フレイビン、ロバート・モリスなど60年代のミニマル・アートの作品群はシンプルさ、フォーマルの持つ力、そして明白さというものを分析的に再定義し、蘇らせた。それは私にとって何よりも勝るモダニズム研究のための導入部を提供してくれていたのだろう。この頃の私はコルビジェのギリシャ寺院とオーシャンライナーの比喩はよく知っていたにもかかわらず、歴史的古典主義とモダニズムの領域の間にまだ何の関係も見いだすことができないでいた。結局先に述べたように、当時は歴史的解釈などモダニズムには何の益もなさないどころか、むしろ邪魔だと考えられていたのである。

その後ランドスケープ・アーキテクチュアにおける古典、そして近代をめぐるデザイン理論（学問として、そして実験的アプローチとして）を探る試みの中で、私は次の二つの流れを見いだした。前近代の時代を貫いて脈打つヨーロッパ・ランドスケープの生成過程に関わる二つの流れである。まず第一に集落や都市から外に広がっていった農業開発の結果としての農村風景がある。これらの風景は、19世紀初期の知的巨人であるジェファーソンやルードンなどに至るまで、文章や批評の対象として存在していた。建築、肖像画の背景も同じ頃には野生の自然から農村風景へと姿を変えていったのである。イギリスやアメリカにおいては20世紀になっても、ピクチャレスクの作庭法とは農業的発想と同列に論じられるものであり、その思惟には美学的考察も含まれていた。

もう一つの流れは、建築的な特質の延長としてである。15世紀に姿を現してきた屋外空間は、庭師の助けを借りながらも、もっぱら建築家によってデザインされた。それらは一般には、小部屋のような空間、テラス、階段やその他の建築的装飾の形をとり、石、舗装、石像のようにあつかわれたトピアリーなどから構成されていた。そして以上二つの流れが互いに歩み寄るには18世紀にフランスやイギリスにおいて公園設置のための運動が始まるまで待たなければならなかった。

しかし今現在の状況を顧みるに、ピクチャレスク風のデザイン・アプローチが、それ以前300年の伝統を持つ整形幾何学的なアプローチを凌駕しているように思える。専門の教育を受けていない現代人にとって、ピクチャレスク的景観は、人間の創り出した芸術ではなく、自然そのものにみえるのだ。

この絵画趣味はル・ノートルの業績をはじめとする偉大な宮城庭園を隅に追いやってきた。かわりにイギリス風景式庭園が、'自然'を象徴しているという理由で、整形庭園よりモダニズム的だとされたのである。オルムステッドによりこのような考え方が確立され、工業化社会の都市が抱える病理的現象への療法として、公園は位置づけられるにいたった。イアン・マクハーグもまたフランス、そしてルネサンス庭園を攻撃する根拠としてこの考え方の上に立っている。しかしながら私の立場はこうである。すなわちこれら整形庭園の方がピクチャレスク庭園よりもむしろ古典的だとさえいえないだろうか。それらの庭園は明らかに12-13世紀に端を発する農業景観の最も高度で洗練され形を表現している。フランス（後にはイギリスでも）の農村風景の再構築は地方での耕作を通して大聖堂の建設を進めようという教会の目論見により成し遂げられたのだが、ル・ノートルの庭園のなかに生け垣、森、低湿地を使った池、そしてフランスの田園風景に固有な直線的な幾何学形態を見いだすことは簡単である。彼の庭園はもちろんフランス整形式庭園もまたピクチャレスク庭園がそうであるのと同じように、自然というものの古典的表現ではないのか。

ところでアジアにおいては庭園は建築とも農業とも違う一種の芸術形態であるとみなされてきた。それはどちらかというと絵画、彫刻、音楽、詩歌と同列に考えられていたようである。庭園は建築よりさらに高度な形態であるとみなされ、そしてそのための形態言語やさまざまなスケールにわたる表現方法が創り出されてきた。これら東洋の庭園の成熟と洗練の過程は多くの点で西洋古典建築のそれと共通するものがある。

先進的なランドスケープ・デザインの作品のいくつかは、構成主義、シューレアリズムなどからの正当たるアプローチを示しているが、モダニズムはいまだランドスケープ・デザインの理論の中に確固とした地位をなしていない。

1920年代フランスにおけるごく短い庭園運動を除いて、デ・スティル、バウハウス、そしてCIAMでさえランドスケープ・デザインを本質的で第一義的な問題であるとは考えていなかった。オープンスペースや自然というものは建築という作品を据えるための空地であるととらえられ、単に量的なものとして扱われていた。言い換えれば彼らはオープンスペースそのものがデザインされるべき対象であるとは認めてなかったのであり、それは中性的環境としてギャラリーや美術館の白い壁となんら変わるところはなかったのである。もっとも現代のモダニズム建築家はどちらかというともっとロマンチックな眼でもってランドスケープを見ていて、無垢の自然ないしは柔らかい優しげな環境として捉えているのかも知れないが、ともあれ1930年代後半、初期のモダニズム建築家達はドイツや他のヨーロッパ諸国を脱出し、アメリカの大学で教鞭をとることになった。そしてそれがモダニズム建築とランドスケープ・デザインの最初の出会いであったといえようか。

私がこの20年間やろうとしてきたことは次の3つの要素を撚り合わせていくことであった。私なりに理解したいわゆる古典主義というもの、西洋や東洋の庭園の持つフォルマリズム、そして後期モダニズムや今世紀中葉のミニマリストたちが同様に持っていたフォルマリズム的性質。これらの結実が私の考えるランドスケープ・デザインにおけるミニマリズムである。

ランドスケープ・デザインにおけるミニマリズム

1960年代のある時期、あるグループの起こした動きは、「ランドスケープの中のミニマリズム」としてアートの世界においてもはっきりと特定できるものであった。その動きは私に初期モダニズムが持っていた分析的関心の再現を思い起こさせた。フォーマルの再発見、精神的支柱としての原初的純粋性及び人間性の意義への希求、神秘そして非参照性への興味、これらはまたいろいろな意味で古典主義の理想にも通ずるものである。

ミニマリズムという言葉と思想、それはちょうど古典主義の場合と同じように、今日の社会の早い流れの中に幾多の芸術的、社会的規範によって再定義を繰り返してきた。しかし大きなコンテクストで見た場合、ミニマリストは自然を知性で、技術で、そして工業力で征服しようと言う態度に一貫して拒否表明を示してきたことがわかる。幾何学的に、また物語として、リズム、ジェスチャーなどを用いて彼らは刻々と移りゆく変幻自在の自然のリアリティやその概念的秩序を指し示そうとし、心に残る空間体験を創り出そうとした。

私は広い意味でミニマリズムという言葉を使っているが、その芸術運動の中核を成す人々の言葉もきわめて示唆に富んでいる。たとえばドナルド．ジャッドは、まずコンテクストや特定の解釈を与えることなく客観的立場に立ち、事物そのものを見つめると云うことを主張する。観客の幾人かは彼ら自身の歴史的、イコン的な投影を投げかけるにしてもミニマリスト的ランドスケープはその根底において何物も参照しないし、何物をも代弁しない。彼らの照準は常にデザインされたランドスケープ、その空間そのもの、そこに内在するエネルギーに合わされている。ミニマリスト・ランドスケープは、より大きい環境の文脈の中にこそ存在するといえるだろう。中断という手法をとるにしても、相互干渉作用に着目するにしても、それを見る目はデザインされた"もの"を超えて風景そのものに向けられている。その際、スケールというものが実際の相対的状況においても個人的、内面的な経験の中においても非常に大きな意味をもってこよう。ただミニマリスト・ランドスケープは絵画や彫刻に見られるように必ずしも本質的に抑制的ではないし、ある必要もない、ということは言っておきたい。ただいくつかの作品は、文字どおりミニマルな要素の使用によってシンプルで直接的な表現を可能にしていることは確かであるが。

ランドスケープ・デザインにおけるミニマリズムは、現代社会の機械化された日常生活の中で進みつつあるクラフトマンシップの喪失、伝統的素材から合成物への移行、スケール感の拡張などの過渡的状況に対処する手がかりを与えてくれる。この観点から次の事に期待できるのではないか。二つの差し迫った環境問題―枯渇する一方の資源、そして増大する一方の廃棄物の山―に対してミニマリズムは芸術的観点からなんらかの満足すべきアプローチを見いだすことが出来るだろう、と言うことである。

ランドスケープ・デザインにおけるミニマリズムへの関心は現在この時点においてまことに的を得たものに思える。いわゆるポストモダンの時代といわれる中で近年のランドスケープ・アーキテクチュア、建築、都市デザインの諸々の作品はモダニズム自体の妥当性について疑問を投げかけ、その幾つかの事例は古典主義への回帰をあらわしたものもある。ではそこで古典主義的デザインについてもっと突っ込んだ新鮮な議論がなされているかと云うとそうでもなく、ほとんどの作品や思考は形式ばったものか装飾的な側面に気をとられているか、そうでなければ社会的、機能的な事柄への関心に終始している。ところがそう云った一連の流れとは別に、視覚芸術の領域の中におけるモダニズム全盛期最後の証としてのミニマリズムの中には、古典主義との共通項が色濃く存在しているようで非常に興味深い。装飾、もしくは機能の追求よりも、ミニマリストはモダニズムと古典主義とを結ぶ何かを追求し、そこに存在する互いに本質的なものを抽象

化し、抽出する事を目指しているのではないだろうか。

ここで第一次世界大戦の始まる前、若き日のル・コルビジェが１９１１年に中近東、地中海地方を旅し、その質の高さ、虚飾を誇らない禁欲的な姿ゆえに、トルコのモスク、ビザンチンの修道院、ブルガリアの民家などに深い感銘を受けたことを思い出してみるのも興味深いだろう。ついにアテネのアクロポリスにおいてその純粋な形態を前にし、彼は畏怖の念に打ちのめされた。形態の昇華とでもいうべき正に普遍的なるものの究極の産物として、それは紛れもない傑作であった。彼の行き着いた結論はこうであった。そこからもう何も差し引くことの出来ない完全な状態、これこそを古典というべきではないか、と。1970年代にル・ノートルのヴォー・ル・ビコンテ、ヴェルサイユ、シュノーなどの庭園に接したとき、私は彼と同様の感慨にふけった。特にそれらの庭園形態の集大成としてのシャンティーユ城は偉大なる石と水と空間、そして光の庭園であり、その形態は昇華され、一つの完成の域にまで高められていた。その庭園は古典であると同時に、またミニマリズム的でもあると私には感じられたのである。

アメリカ環境デザインにおけるモダニズムの全盛期に遭遇した私というひとりのランドスケープ・アーキテクトの、ここに述べてきたことは個人的な内面の軌跡である。いくつもの庭園、風景をはじめ、その他一般デザイン、芸術家の作品、彼らの洞察などを通して、私はものの見方を学び、私自身の進むべき道を模索してきた。やすらぎに満ち、ゴミゴミしておらず、しかも同時にとても表現的で示唆に富んでいる―そんな環境の創造へのアプローチこそ私が探していた道であり、人類の歴史の中でも現在特に必要とされているものではないだろうか。これこそが私が個人として出来る何かではないか。今まさに混迷を深めつつある中で、精神的価値を失い、手入れもされず、そして詰め込まれ過ぎの庭園―地球のなかで、それでも私たちは孤独にひたれる場所を探し、集う場所を欲し、新しく発見されるに値する場を、何よりも住むにふさわしい場所を求めているのだ。

アートは庭園足り得るか？

アートの一鑑賞者から、それらに対するアイデアとランドスケープ・デザインとを結びつけられないかという考えにいたるのには少々時間が必要であった。まず私はいわゆるアート収集家であり、ギャラリーに頻繁に顔を出し、特にミニマリストに関する本、雑誌、カタログを貪欲に漁った。専門的な知識があってのことでもなく、またほかの領域との関連など思いもかけず、ただ単に美しいものを楽しむだけであった。ただ純粋にアートが持つ美と意味、それらがはらむ視覚的、知的エネルギーに興味があったのであろう。

私が、フランク・ステラのストライプを描いたペインティングの中に初めてランドスケープ的なアイデアを見出したのは数年の後のことであった。パターンそれ自体のデザインが、いかに絵画（または壁画）そのもののかたちを規定し、フレームの存在を不要にし、そして抽象化されたイメージとして読みとられることを拒んでいたか。壁によって周囲から切りとられてもいないのに、それはまるで空間として意味を持ちつつ私たちの眼前に存在する庭園のようであった。

カール・アンドレの「敷き詰められた金属片」は庭園の強烈なメタファーに思える。ほとんど３次元的要素のない平面はしかしその上に広がる空間を完全にコントロールしている。それは私に砂漠の民ベドウィンのペルシャ絨毯、即ちどこへでも持ち運べる理想的な居心地のよい庭を、思い出させた。同じく彼の「１４４個のブロックと石」という作品もまたそのアイデアを見事に具体化していた。そこでは全ての壁（建築）は空虚な空間であり、その床（ランドスケープ）は複雑で謎めき、シンボルやゲーム性に満ちたものであった。使っている素材は本当に目立たない、ありふれたものだがその作品がもたらすものは力強く、私はそこに庭園が本来持っているべきミステリアスな魂の存在を感じたものである。　同じくカール・アンドレの「割線」という作品は何の変哲もない野原におかれた。そこは確かに美しい自然であるが、取り立てて目立つと云う程のものでもなかった。しかし全くシンプルに材木を並べただけで、その場所は人々が集う場所となり、意識的にしろ無意識にしろ決して忘れることの出来ない特別な場へと変容を遂げたのである。

柔らかくうねるカリフォルニア特有の丘陵地の上をマリン、ソノマ州を横切って太平洋に至るまで設置されたクリストによる「ランニング・フェンス」もまた同様である。単なるフェンスがランドスケープを祝祭の場へと変えた。この地域の風景は私が育ち人生のほとんどを過ごした、私にとって最も慣れ親しんだはずの風景であったが、その時ほど私自身が風景の一部であると強く感じたことはなかった。たった一筋のシートが何と驚くべきことを成し遂げることか。正直に云うとその時に及んでなお私は鑑賞者として一連の作品から受けた感動と、私がランドスケープ・アーキテクトとして考え、実行すべきことの間に何の直接的な関係も見いだせずにいた。

その後もより多くの作品に接し、私は次第に単なる収集家として以上のことをそれらの作品に求めて行くようになっていった。そしてついに私は自分自身が単なる収集家であることに我慢がならなくなったのである。私が庭園を全く新しい方法でつくってみようという直接のきっかけになったのは1970年代終わりのある夏、フランス庭園へのツアーにおいてであった。偉大なる歴史を持つ整形式庭園、ミニマリストのアート、そして私自身がずっと持っていたランドスケープへのビジョンがこのとき初めて結びついたといえよう。その試みはまず非常に実験的なものから始められた。しかし単にギャラリーや特定の場所でのアートとしてのアイデアをランドスケープ・

デザインに引用してきても、それはあまりうまく機能しなかったし、ましてや新しい方向性を示す訳でもないことが次第に明らかになってきた。というのもランドスケープ・アーキテクチュアには自然との関わりがもたらす多様な次元があり、それら全てがデザインの中に包含されねばならないからである。

ただ事物を対象化させるというアイデアそのものはランドスケープ・デザインにおいても有効であった。例えば、ある意味を浮き彫りにして対象化させるという考えはそれに伴う飽くなき思考過程から切り放して考えることは出来ないという考え方、など。ランドスケープの中に置かれたオブジェ、あるいはあるオーダーに従ったシステムは、それが置かれた場所とだけではなくその周りの全てのもの、即ち太陽や月の運行、季節ごとの光の違い、温度変化、そして生成死滅を繰り返す生命そのものなどとつながり、かつ強烈な対比をなす。そして初めて「それ」として、はっきり認識されるのである。自然と、最も単純なオブジェとの間にさえ存在する複雑極まる相互関係は、特定の敷地での作品制作へ向けての我々の想像を増幅、拡大する。そしてここにきて時間という概念が場所そのものと同じくらい重要な要因として浮かび上がってくる。

この認識は概念としては一般に分かりやすい当たり前のことをいってるようだが、その意味の明白さにおいて私にとってはきわめて斬新なものであった。しかし現代ランドスケープデザインの分野においては、時間の要素と現実の非予測性はデザイン上の重要な問題としては扱われてこなかったのである。それには次に挙げる三つのデカルト的理性が関わっていると思われる。第一に科学的、技術的手法は自然そのものの神秘さを讃えるよりも、むしろそれを圧倒し、コントロールし、部分に還元しようとする傾向を持つということ。次に私たちは環境デザインの専門家として、自然がもつ複雑さとその変化に対応する術も意志も持ち合わせていないこと。自然を機械的かつ予測可能なものとして扱おうという態度があまりにも高く位置づけられているのではないか。三つめは、モダニズム思想の誤った受けとり方に起因するディテール、特定のプログラムに対する過度の思い込み。もしも形態が機能に従うならば、かたちを生み出すための機能の分析が最優先されるだろう。形態は単なる機能の表現型となり、結果としてデザインが目指すべきゴールとは自ずから異なるものとなる。もっと直観的な芸術的手法や、ごく一般的で普遍的なプログラムの方が、人間の営みと変化し続ける世界との間から素晴らしいものを取り出して表現するのによほど向いている、と私は考えるのだが。

核となるアイデアは身近に満ちあふれているのに、一体どれが有効に、適切に、美しく、そして神秘的かつ精神的に世界と共鳴するのかを選び出すパラメーターが未だ見つかっていない。ランドスケープ・アーキテクチュアに関する概念的、現実的思考における問題の本質はこうであろう。

当時のモダニスト・ランドスケープ・デザイナーにはまだ気付かれていなかったが、ミニマルアートとありのままの自然を組み合わせるという思いもよらないコンビネーションは、その問題を解くための新しい試みや実験のための素晴らしい可能性を提供してくれていた。この新しいものの見方は庭園や都市のプラザなど正統的な対象だけでなく、あらゆる公共空間、放棄された空地、街路、駐車場、屋上など全てに及ぶ啓示であった。だけでなく、それは新旧にわたる市街地、郊外をもう一度見直す際の良き基準ともなったのである。

自立性

それが対象としてはっきりと存在を認められ、その意味までもが認知されるためには、それ自身が自立していなければならない。もしそれが建物や彫刻に従属するものであったり、現前する既存の風景と混同されるものだったりすれば、その作品は自らを表現し、意味を与え、物語を生みだし、私たちの記憶の中に刻印されるだけの力に欠けるということである。高度に手入れされた装飾的な庭園さえ、他の芸術作品に比して同等に客観的対象として存在し得なければ、改めて私たちの目を向けさせることは出来ないのだ。

いま現代社会は断片化、商業化の流れにいる。大多数にとって風景はただ外に広がる空虚である。現代都市のオープンスペースは端に押しやられ、取り残され、見捨てられている。都市の人々にとって記念されるべきシンボルは朽ち果てた。自然の、そして歴史の、あるいは遠く離れた場所の映像が次々とリアルな屋外での体験にとって変わっていく。このような状況の中において、風景の自立にとって何が可能なのだろうか。

断片化は物理的にも心理的にも、私たちの自然な秩序感覚を壊していく。流れはせき止められ、暗渠につながれる。丘陵や山々は切り崩されてすでに姿を消したか、もしくはいまだその傷口をさらし出している。人々が歩ける場所は寸断されてしまった。建物群と化学的汚染が敷地の本来の姿を見えなくしているが、それは海や、そして空についてもいえることである。ロス・アンジェルス盆地、マンハッタン島、ボストンのチャールズ・リバーなど数え切れないほどの特徴ある自然景観が道路、建物、あるいは恣意的に造られた景観によって、侵食されている。

この風景の奇形化の底に横たわるものは、山や、平原、湖、河川や海、そして農業や小さな集落の景観に対して前近代の人々が見いだした秩序、静けさ、視覚的規範の欠落、及び安定感の喪失である。その時代状況の中では、私たちの住んでいる場所の空間的秩序は、より大きな自然界を参照していたといえる。それは全体としての地球との関係性を模倣するものでもあった。

もしもシンプルな秩序が断片化、周縁化、細断化と明快なコントラストを成すならば、抑制と

絞り込むことの価値は私たちの文化にある種の方向性を与え得るだろう。音楽的リズムの連続や反復、幾何学的パターン（特に線形及び点状グリッド）など多くのミニマル・アートや伝統的な整形式庭園に見られる秩序だての道具は他にも、空間の知覚的拡大や連続する線形パターンによる空間表現、左右対称または非対称によるバランスを生み出す空間のエッジや中心の積極的な活用、などが挙げられる。テクスチュアとパターンの探求や、スケール、色の対比といった手法もまた、人工ー自然、生命ー非活性の対比などと共に秩序形成への手がかりとなる。記念、物語性、そして象徴性もまた上記のリストに加わりうるだろう。視覚領域がもつ根元的な力を取り戻すための分析が必要とされる中、最も必要とされるのは皮肉を込めることではなく、土地の持つ神秘性そのものを導き出すことにある。

アートとしてのランドスケープ

オープンスペースは現代市民社会の中で、内部空間と同等もしくはそれ以上の重要性を持っている。それは建築的装飾やファサードと同じ様にモニュメンタルかつミステリアスなものであり得る。機能的に、しかし美的には失われたも同然の街路や駐車場、ビルの裏口などに囲まれた公共オープンスペースの現状には、無関心がもたらした醜さに目を覆うべきものがあり、初期のモダニズムが掲げていた合理性への希求が失敗に終わったことを如実に示している。明かにモダニズムが招いた失敗のほとんどは街の公共空間、オープンスペースに現れており、そして失敗の原因はそれらの敷地計画そのものの中にあったといえるだろう。

　古典建築のテーマの一つに、自然に立ち戻り言及し直す行為を通じて完全なる理想的形態を追求するという態度があったことを考えてみたいと思う。その態度及びそこからの生成物は、より広がりを見せ豊かになっていく文化的コンテクストとともに幾世代にもわたる発明、再評価、時代ごとの表現方法などと互いに織り合わさりながら熟成してきた。ここで一つの疑問が浮かんでくる。では私達はいかにしてそれ自身が既に自然の一部であるランドスケープ・アートに自然そのものと匹敵するものを見いだせるのだろうか。

　そのカギを自然を二つの方向から見てみることから得られないだろうか。一つは野生としての自然、そしてもう一つは飼い慣らされ、コントロールされた自然である。

　野生の自然、そして広大なランドスケープは決して古典建築に示唆されるような安定性、永続性を持つものではない。従って建築的な思考はおそらく私たちランドスケープ・アーキテクトが求めている概念とは相入れないものだと云わざるを得ないだろう。音楽はしばしばランドスケープの比喩として用いられるがこれはあまりにも一過性に過ぎる。音楽はまた空間そのものにも例えられるが（ジョン・ケージの音楽の様に）それは決して空間のように物理的に人を受け入れるものではない。オープンスペースとは様々な影響を私たちに与える非常に複雑な媒体である。常に錯綜する変化の状態にあり、日毎、季節毎、生成の周期と共に変化し、匂い、音、雨、乾燥などが絡まりあい複雑極まる様相をなす。それは芸術の対象としては最も私たちの生活そのものの複雑さと比肩しうるものであろう。

　変化し続ける自然という存在は、他の芸術領域とは違った形でのもう一つの芸術のあり方を示唆しているのではないだろうか。今現在そのことに対する取り組みは未だ創造の途上にあり、同時に将来に向けての発展、拡大、対話、そして望むべくには私たちの進むべき方向とその希望にも開かれている。

　とは言ってもここで考えなければいけない問題はたくさんある。現代の風景とは（自然にしろ都会的なものにしろ）扱うには野性的すぎはしないか。私たちは実際のところ本当にそれを芸術作品にすることが出来るのだろうか。風景という概念は現代社会の複雑さの中に十分な意味付けをもたらすことが出来るのか。言葉を換えれば、これらの問題意識は私たちが探し求めるゴールへと続いているのかどうか。私はそれは可能だと信じる。ルイス・バラガン、イサム・ノグチ、ブルーノ・マルクス、ダン・カイリー、ローレンス・ハルプリンをはじめとして、この時代に登場した多くの偉大なランドスケープ・デザイナーたちの革新的な仕事がそれを物語っている。そしてミニマリズムとは、私たちの文化が待ち望んでいる解決策を探り当てるための手がかりの一つである。私にはそう思えてならない。